FLY THE W

The Chicago Cubs' Historic 2016 Championship Season

Daily Herald

dh dailyherald.com

(John Starks/Daily Herald)

This book is available in quantity at special discounts for your group or organization. For further information, contact:

Triumph Books LLC
814 North Franklin Street
Chicago, Illinois 60610
Phone: (312) 337-0747
www.triumphbooks.com

Printed in U.S.A.
ISBN: 978-1-62937-444-4

Daily Herald
Douglas K. Ray: Chairman, Publisher and CEO
Scott T. Stone: President/Chief Operating Officer
Colin M. O'Donnell: Senior Vice President/Director of Content
John Lampinen: Senior Vice President/Editor
Jim Baumann: Vice President/Managing Editor
Tom Quinlan: Assistant Managing Editor/Sports
Contributors: Bruce Miles, Mike Imrem, Barry Rozner, Travis Siebrass, Tim Broderick, Jeff Knox, Joe Lewnard, Mark Welsh, Daniel White, Steve Lundy, Brian Hill, Morgan Timms

Interior Design: Patricia Frey
Cover Design: Andy Hansen
Front cover foreground image by John Starks/Daily Herald. Front flap photo by Patrick Kunzer/Daily Herald. Back flap photo Joe Lewnard/Daily Herald. Front cover "W" image and back cover image by AP Images.

This is an unofficial publication. This book is in no way affiliated with, licensed by or endorsed by Major League Baseball or the Chicago Cubs.

(John Starks/Daily Herald)

Contents

Foreword

A Lifetime of Memories in One Spectacular Chicago Cubs Season

By Len Kasper

This was simply the most fun spring, summer and fall of baseball I have ever witnessed. The memories, moments and oddities are flooding my brain, in no particular order …

Embracing the target, the Mother's Day marathon, the Kris Bryant game, Jake Arrieta's no-hitter, the pennant-clincher by Kyle Hendricks, Kyle Schwarber's devastating injury and subsequent miraculous return.

Dexter Fowler's surprise re-signing, all-star season and Game 7 leadoff homer.

Addison Russell's dives and his Game 6 grand slam, Javier Baez's hands, lightning-quick tags and his MLB tattoo, Willson Contreras' energy, Travis Wood's catch in the ivy on national television and October home run.

David Ross' throws, sense of humor and Game 7 home run.

Anthony Rizzo's ledge catch. And his leadership. And his charitable heart.

Jason Heyward's professionalism. And his defense.

Rob Zastryzny's last name. And Matt Szczur's too.

Szczur's bat. And his underwear.

Police escorts to the ballparks and airports.

Ben Zobrist's walk-up music. And his MVP Series.

Ryan Kalish's inspirational, albeit brief, return, Munenori Kawasaki's spring training home run.

John Lackey's facial expressions, Jon Lester's scowls, and his work ethic.

Miguel Montero's tweets and his championship series grand slam.

Pat Hughes' iconic pennant-clinching and World Series-winning radio calls, Ron Coomer's laugh and Jim Deshaies' one-liners.

Kris Bryant's versatility. And his baserunning. And power. And his infectious smile. And his All-Star Game home run off Chris Sale.

Fans fly the W following the Cubs' NLCS Game 6 victory. (Steve Lundy/Daily Herald)

Pedro Strop's crooked cap. And his quick pitch, Carl Edwards Jr.'s skinny frame, and ridiculous stuff.

Chris Bosio's no-nonsense interviews, bullpen coach Lester Strode's class and positivity, and strength coach Tim Buss' inspirational pre-team stretch speeches.

Billy Williams' batting cage observations, and Ryne Sandberg in the stands wearing his Cubs hat.

Aroldis Chapman's fastball, Hector Rondon's slider, and Mike Montgomery's World Series-clinching save.

Bob Newhart's tweets, Jason Hammel's beard, and Beanie Maddon's police escort to Game 3.

Jake Arrieta's beard, his flat-brimmed cap, and his flawless posture.

A jam-packed Clark Street before, during and after the NLCS clincher.

Tom Ricketts' commitment and Cubs fans' undying loyalty.

Theo Epstein's contract extension, and his fake mustache.

The immortal spirit and legacy of Ron Santo and Ernie Bank.

Wrigley Field under the lights with a packed house going bonkers. And in the quiet mornings before the gates open.

Joe's Maddonisms. Respect 90. Try not to suck. Never permit the pressure to exceed the pleasure. Do simple better.

Kyle Hendricks' major-league leading earned run average. And his steely demeanor.

Eddie Vedder cheering from the front row, Jeff Garlin and Bill Murray singing the stretch, and Eddie's duet with Harry.

Hendricks' devastating changeup. Lester's cutter and competitiveness, Arrieta's slider and home run power.

John's Vincent singing our national anthem, Julianna Zobrist's "God Bless America," and Wayne Messmer's voice.

All the crazy themed road trips.

John Mallee's work ethic and Mike Borzello's game plans. Gary Jones' toothpick, and his gutsy sends.

Brandon Hyde playing catch with his son Colton in the outfield.

Javier Baez's homer vs. the Giants, Addison Russell's blast in Los Angeles and their pennant-clinching double play.

Albert Almora Jr.'s defensive instincts.

Postgame celebrations. Post-series celebrations.

October, color-changing ivy.

25-6, 47-20, 103-58.

22-6 in August.

656 walks and 808 runs.

Plus-252 run differential.

A 3.15 team ERA.

Eliminating the Giants in their own ballpark.

Beating Clayton Kershaw for a trip to the World Series.

Cubs baseball in November.

Game 7. All of it in its wacky, heart-wrenching glory.

AC 0000000.

National League Central Champions, National League pennant winners for the first time in 71 years, World Series Champions for the first time in 108 years. **WS**

Len Kasper is in his 12th season as the television play-by-play voice for the Chicago Cubs. Follow him on Twitter @LenKasper.

The Chicago Cubs celebrate becoming World Series champions for the first time since 1908. (John Starks/Daily Herald)

Introduction

A World Series Tribute to Old Chicago Cubs and Die-Hard Fans

By Bruce Miles, dailyherald.com | November 3, 2016

Who is this one for? First and foremost, the Cubs' World Series championship is for the fans.

That's something team chairman Tom Ricketts acknowledged right away Wednesday night, minutes after the Cubs outlasted the Cleveland Indians 8-7 in 10 innings to win Game 7 of the World Series.

"The Cubs, as a team, they're a member of your family," Ricketts said. "And like all members of the family, you love them, but sometimes they let you down. Maybe they might let you down for 100 years in a row. And we did. We didn't close the deal. And now, just tell everyone thank you and this is for you."

But this one is for a lot of other people, too, some living and some not.

This one is for Mr. Cub, Ernie Banks, who rode the wave in 1969 only to see it come crashing down on him and the Cubs late in the season.

Ernie, who died in 2015, never appeared in a postseason game. And you know exactly what his spirit is saying after the Cubs captured their first World Series since 1908: "Let's win two."

This one is for Ernie's teammate, Ron Santo. One can only imagine Ronnie shouting, "Yes! Yes!" after

another third baseman, Kris Bryant, threw to first for the final out.

This one is for Billy Williams, he of the sweet swing and the sweeter disposition. After the Cubs clinched the pennant at Wrigley Field by beating the Dodgers, Billy stood in left field, the field he patrolled for so long, and called it "sacred ground." May Billy see several more of these.

This one is for Jack Brickhouse, who no doubt looked down and gave a big "Hey Hey!" I started thinking about Jack late in the game, remembering it also was in Cleveland where he called the White Sox's pennant clincher in 1959. Nobody saw more bad Cubs baseball than Jack, but he was a ray of sunshine every afternoon.

This one is for Harry Caray, who no doubt is toasting one and bellowing "Holy cow!" I remember Harry's eyes tearing up at the end of one season. He broadcast World Series wins for the Cardinals, but never for the Cubs.

This one is for Vince Lloyd and Lou Boudreau. Like Brickhouse on TV, they were your Cubs companions on the radio side, with Vince giving it the "Holy mackerel!" after every big play. Lou had ties to both the

(Daniel White/Daily Herald)

Cubs and Indians, who honor him with a special place in Progressive Field.

This one is for Phil Cavarretta, the Chicago boy who played on the 1945 pennant winners, the last team before this year's club to make it to the World Series. Phil wore No. 44, a number carried on with honor today by fellow first baseman Anthony Rizzo.

This one is for Gabby Hartnett, whose "homer in the gloamin'" helped the Cubs to the 1938 pennant.

This one is for "Jolly Cholly," Charlie Grimm. The left-handed banjo player played for, managed and broadcast for the Cubs. When the Cubs acquired reliever Justin Grimm, us old-timers told him he had the perfect name for a Cub.

This one is for Hall of Famer Ryne Sandberg, who was welcomed back into the organization and was able to enjoy this World Series run in person. Pure class.

This one is for the Hawk, Sut, the Sarge and Bobby D.

This one is for Fergie Jenkins and Greg Maddux, a pair of Hall of Fame No. 31s who threw out ceremonial first pitches at Wrigley Field.

This one is for Kerry Wood, who fell short in Game 7 of the 2003 NLCS and remains an ambassador for the club. It was good to see him in the clubhouse Wednesday. In all the years I covered Kerry, we never had a bad word between us.

This one is for modern-day warrior Ryan Dempster, the face of the Cubs for much of a decade. Woe to anyone who badmouthed the Cubs when they got down against the Dodgers in the NLCS in Demp's presence. The Cubs traded him in 2012, but you'll never take the Cub out of Dempster, and he's now a special assistant to the team.

This one is for Tom "Otis" Hellmann and Gary Stark, the longtime clubhouse guys. They get to the park before everybody and leave after everybody. It was so good to see them reveling in the clubhouse fun Wednesday night. And here's a tip of the white fishing hat to retired clubhouse man Yosh Kawano.

This one is for the execs who tried but couldn't get it done.

Former GM Jim Hendry and his lieutenants brought in Javier Baez and Willson Contreras, and current team president Theo Epstein makes sure to remind people of that.

Hendry's old boss, Andy MacPhail, remains gracious and kind in his current role with the Phillies.

Dallas Green's 1984 team came within a fingertip of the World Series.

But Tom Ricketts had it right in the first place: This one's for you. **WS**

World Series

(Brian Hill/Daily Herald)

The Biggest Stage

Cubs Not Down or Out After Game 1 Defeat

By Barry Rozner, dailyherald.com

Five years ago Tuesday, Theo Epstein stepped in front of a microphone at a Wrigley Field news conference for the first time.

He might as well have been stepping in front of a CTA bus for all the chance people gave him of rebuilding a Cubs organization that had been thrown together like an '80s resale shop.

And yet, Tuesday night at Progressive Field, there were Epstein's Cubs in the World Series, arriving in Cleveland near the top of the mountain, a step below the summit, and knowing the toughest part of the climb awaited.

There was pomp, circumstance and frivolity, not to mention Corey Kluber, Andrew Miller and Cody Allen.

The Cubs expected the outside noise, but maybe not the two-seamer inside that Kluber used to baffle Cubs hitters to the tune of 9 strikeouts in 6 innings, outpitching Jon Lester in a 6-0 victory in Game 1 of the World Series.

If that weren't surprising enough, Cleveland catcher Roberto Perez hit 2 home runs, giving him 3 bombs in 27 postseason at-bats, after hitting 3 all season in 153 at-bats.

It was a disappointing opening game for the visitors, leaving 9 on base and going 1-for-11 with runners in scoring position, but there was an ease about the team postgame.

It was a very relaxed Cubs clubhouse, as if they knew something we didn't.

"We've got a confident group here," said veteran David Ross. "We've been down before and we know what we're capable of. Their guy made better pitches than our guy.

"Next game, we'll try to turn that around."

The Indians served notice that they will be no easy out, striking a pose closely resembling the Kansas City Royals of the last few years. They don't appear to do anything great -- except play great fundamental baseball.

Jon Lester was no match for Indians starter Corey Kluber in Game 1 of the World Series. (John Starks/Daily Herald)

And they displayed that to near-perfection in Game 1.

The Cleveland rotation was terrific all summer until injuries took a toll, but they survived because of great defense, a stealth offense and—as of late—a wicked two-man bullpen.

And it took only into the bottom of the first of Game 1 to see how they reached the World Series, scoring twice while barely hitting the ball out of the infield.

They scratch out a few runs early, get the ball to Miller and Allen and put teams away with a frustrating attack that sneaks up on opponents and roughs them up with a dull nail file.

But the Cubs did see Miller for 46 pitches in 2 innings, which can only help in the days ahead, especially for the guys who have never faced him.

And they had Miller on the ropes with the bases loaded and nobody out in the seventh, but Willson Contreras popped out, Addison Russell struck out and Ross went fishing on a 3-2 slider that would have been ball four if he hadn't committed.

They also got the tying run to the plate in the eighth, before Kyle Schwarber swung and missed a pitch he was trying to hit to Toledo, or Akron, or someplace else in Ohio far from here.

"We missed some opportunities late in the game, but I'm proud of our guys and the at-bats we had later

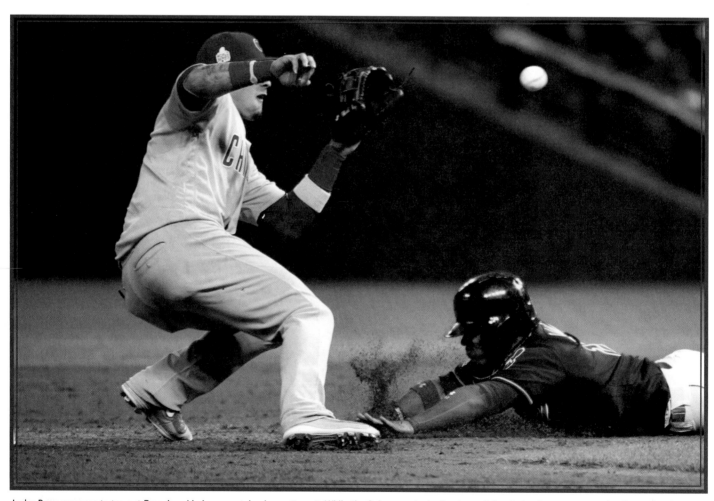

Javier Baez prepares to tag out Francisco Lindor on a stolen base attempt. While the Cubs were typically strong defensively, they were unproductive at the plate. (John Starks/Daily Herald)

Appearing in his first major-league game since April, Kyle Schwarber hits a double in the fourth inning of Game 1. (John Starks/Daily Herald)

in the game," Ross said. "We continued to grind and I think we can take a lot of confidence out of the second half of this game."

To look into their eyes and listen to them talk is to believe that the Cubs are not worried after one game.

"It sounds like a cliché," said Anthony Rizzo with a small grin, "but there's a lot of positives to take out of this. We had some really good at-bats in this game and if we keep doing that we'll be all right."

Yeah, the Cubs have written this script before. They start a series with no offense and then start hitting

when it suits them, as they did against the Giants and Dodgers.

They won Game 1 of the first two series at home, but they were also down 2-1 to the Dodgers on the road for the middle three before winning three straight to capture the pennant in Game 6 at Wrigley Field against Clayton Kershaw.

So they will do what they always do, which is come to the park with a plan for Trevor Bauer and expect to win Wednesday.

Panic is simply not part of the program. **WS**

WORLD SERIES » GAME 2

October 26, 2016 • Cleveland, Ohio • Cubs 5, Indians 1

In the Books

Schwarber's Spark Gets Chicago Cubs Going

By Bruce Miles, dailyherald.com

Kyle Schwarber may be taking baby steps in his recovery from knee surgery, but his legend is growing by leaps and bounds.

Schwarber added to it Wednesday night, and it again came at a most opportune time for the Chicago Cubs.

He had a pair of run-scoring singles and a walk as the Cubs evened the World Series at one game apiece with a 5-1 victory over the Cleveland Indians at Progressive Field.

Now that they have wrested homefield advantage away from the Indians, the Cubs could win the World Series by taking all three games at home this weekend.

Schwarber, who had 5 home runs in the postseason as a rookie last year, continues to leave baseball people slack-jawed by his exploits.

It wasn't until last week that Schwarber was even cleared to play baseball, and now he finds himself in the World Series. It looks like he has both his swing and his eye at the plate back. It can't be that easy.

"No, it's not that easy, first off," he said. "Baseball's a crazy game. It will do crazy things to you, but this is the moment that we all look for when we were little kids, to play in the World Series and win it. We just took a small step today, but we've still got a long way to go."

What Schwarber's left-handed bat has done is transform the Cubs' lineup. It also has given a spark to a team that would seem not to need one. After all, the Cubs won 103 games in the regular season before beating the Giants and the Dodgers in the National League playoffs.

"You saw, he jacks everybody up," manager Joe Maddon said. "Those couple big hits he got again, really, (teammate Anthony) Riz really responded to it well. The whole group did. It makes your lineup longer."

The Cubs got going quickly against Cleveland starting pitcher Trevor Bauer. With one out in the first inning, Kris Bryant singled and came home on Rizzo's double.

Schwarber's first RBI single came in the third. The Cubs chased Bauer after 3⅔ innings and 87 pitches. They scored three times in the fifth, with Schwarber adding another run-scoring single.

Kyle Schwarber's third-inning RBI single helped the Cubs log their first win to even the series. (John Starks/Daily Herald)

The beneficiary was starting pitcher Jake Arrieta, who got the win by working 5⅔ innings and giving up 2 hits and a run. Arrieta had a no-hitter until giving up a double to Jason Kipnis with one out in the sixth.

The Cubs' starting pitcher, a workout freak of some legend, marveled at Schwarber's rehab from knee surgery he underwent in April after an outfield collision during the first week of the season.

"You just look at Kyle, and we've all watched him continue to progress throughout his rehab, and you can't say enough about him," Arrieta said. "I said this a few days ago, but he's in the training room and the weight room four, five, hours a day. He's in a constant sweat."

He may put Cleveland pitchers into a cold sweat this weekend if doctors clear him to play the outfield. The Cubs will work out Friday at Wrigley Field, and Schwarber may take flyballs in left field to test the knee. So far, he has not been cleared to play the field.

"We'll see where it goes," he said.

It's going back to Wrigley Field, just where Maddon likes it.

"It's always good," he said. It's always crazy good, but I have to imagine a little bit more than that, especially coming back at 1-1. I think the folks will be jacked up about the win tonight. But it's the finest venue in professional sports and maybe in all of sports."

As for Schwarber, he maybe be feeling little or no pain these days. He's certainly feeling no pressure.

"Hey, man, I'm living the dream," he said. "We're playing in the World Series. What else can you ask for? I'm just going to keep riding the wave 'til it ends." **WS**

Willson Contreras is safe at first base after the Indians' Jason Kipnis bobbles the batted ball. With Kyle Schwarber injured for most of the year, Contreras stepped up as a dependable catcher and batter. (John Starks/Daily Herald)

WORLD SERIES » GAME 3

October 28, 2016 • Chicago, Illinois • Inidians 1, Cubs 0

Falling Fast

Indians Shut Out Cubs 1-0 in Game 3

Bruce Miles, dailyherald.com

A rare warm October night, complete with a gusty wind blowing out, greeted the Chicago Cubs and Cleveland Indians Friday at Wrigley Field.

So what did we get on this inviting night for hitting?

A 1-0 victory for Cleveland in Game 3 of the World Series. The Indians own a two-games-to-one lead in the best-of-seven series, and they'll have their ace, Corey Kluber, going on short rest Saturday night in Game 4.

The Indians scored the only run in the seventh inning on a pinch single by Coco Crisp. The Cubs now have been shut out four times in the postseason. They had runners on second and third with two outs in the bottom of the ninth, but Javier Baez struck out to end the game.

The wind blowing out has been rare this year at Wrigley, and it brought with it a comfortable temperature of 62 degrees.

With the Indians starting flyball pitcher Josh Tomlin, it figured to be a good night for Cubs power hitters. But in baseball, there's nothing much that figures.

"I think all the things adding up is like a negative to it," said Cubs first baseman Anthony Rizzo, who was 1-for-4. "The guy is a flyball pitcher, the wind is howling out, it's October. Of course, a 1-0 game and a little broken-bat (hit) to win it. That's the way this game is. You've got to roll with it. You've got to roll with the ups and downs."

The Cubs sent Kyle Hendricks to the mound, and he has done good work at Wrigley. After getting out of a couple of jams early, he could not make it out of the fifth, exiting with the bases loaded and one out, only to be bailed out when reliever Justin Grimm got a double-play ball from Francisco Lindor.

"Just a battle," Hendricks said. "I wasn't sharp, but they had a good game plan against me. They were laying off some good pitches, putting together good AB's. Just didn't have a good feel today for them and myself."

Hendricks, who had a 1.32 ERA at Wrigley Field during the regular season, took note of the elements.

"I try not to think about it too much," he said. "Coming out of the game and then looking back,

Ben Zobrist is unable to spark the Cubs offense during a low-scoring Game 3. (Steve Lundy/Daily Herald)

23

having a 1-0 game with the wind blowing out like that, I don't think you'll see that very often."

Tomlin did just enough for Cleveland, as manager Terry Francona went to his bullpen early, going for ace lefty Andrew Miller in the fifth. Miller got pinch hitter Miguel Montero on a lineout to right and strand a runner on second.

"That bullpen has done an unbelievable job for us all year long," Tomlin said. "And the situation we're in now, pinch hitter coming up, that's probably your best option. I get it."

Cubs manager Joe Maddon said his hitters just need to recalibrate after striking out eight times.

"I thought it was a well-played game," Maddon said. "I thought we played great defense again tonight. We were just out of the (strike) zone way too often."

The Cubs had chances in each of the final three innings. In the seventh, Jorge Soler tripled on a high flyball down the right field line. He was slow to get out of the box, saying through a translator he thought the ball was going foul but that the wind pushed it

back into play. Indians right fielder Lonnie Chisenhall jumped for the ball but could not get it.

Baez grounded out to end that threat. Dexter Fowler singled with two outs in the eighth but Kris Bryant struck out. In the ninth, Rizzo singled to lead off. Chris Coghlan pinch ran for him. Ben Zobrist struck out, and Willson Contreras grounded out, sending Coghlan to second. After Jason Heyward reached first base on an error and stole second base, Baez struck out against Cody Allen.

The crowd of 41,703 filed out quietly, but the fans made a lot of noise early in the first World Series game at Wrigley Field since 1945. Zobrist, who helped the Royals win the World Series last year, didn't seem to think the Cubs were too amped up.

"The crowd was awesome," he said. "They were fantastic all game long. Everybody had a good time, it seemed like. Obviously we all wanted the outcome to be different, but they were great, and it was electric out there. It would have been nice to get them a 'W,' but we'll do that tomorrow." **WS**

Top: Wrigley Field is prepped for its first World Series game since 1945, though the Cubs failed to record a win in Game 3. Opposite: Catcher Willson Contreras throws to Javier Baez at second base. (Steve Lundy/Daily Herald)

WORLD SERIES » GAME 4

October 29, 2016 • Chicago, Illinois • Indians 7, Cubs 2

Backs Against the Wall

Cubs on Brink of Season Ending After 7-2 Loss

Bruce Miles, dailyherald.com

The Cleveland Indians may have been the most overlooked team in all of the playoffs this October.

Now they're one victory away from being World Series champions.

And they're doing it at the expense of the Chicago Cubs.

After playing a National League game Friday night and beating the Cubs 1-0, the American League champs played some AL ball Saturday night, beating the Cubs 7-2 at Wrigley Field to take a 3-1 lead in the Series.

If the Cubs want to send the Series back to Cleveland, they'll need staff ace Jon Lester to rescue them Sunday night in Game 5.

"Especially with Jonny going, this is going to sound cliché, but we feel good about it," said first baseman Anthony Rizzo. "We're down 3-1 in the World Series. We get tomorrow and we really put pressure on them. It's about focusing right away."

The Indians ace, Corey Kluber, demonstrated both guts and guile in Game 4. Pitching on three days rest,

Kluber worked 6 innings, giving up 5 hits and 1 run while throwing 81 pitches.

Kluber's counterpart, Cubs starter John Lackey, threw 84 pitches in 5 innings as he gave up 4 hits and 3 runs.

The Cubs even scored first in this one. Dexter Fowler led off the bottom of the first with a double. After Kris Bryant popped out, Rizzo singled Fowler home.

But that was about it for the Cubs, who again could get little going. Kluber's breaking pitches were especially effective against right-handed hitters as he struck out six.

"They were definitely more aggressive this time around," said Kluber, who is 2-0 in the World Series and has an 0.89 ERA in the entire postseason. "But that's how most lineups approach me, so it wasn't anything we had to figure out on the fly."

The Cubs and manager Joe Maddon had hoped to bring a better approach at the plate. But Kluber was too much for what still is a young and sometimes anxious

Starter John Lackey watches Jose Ramirez's home run ball disappear over the fence in the second inning of Game 4. (John Starks/Daily Herald)

lineup. Cubs batters walked once and struck out eight times for the game.

"They don't walk a lot of people because they get a lot of chases," Bryant said. "If we're able to do that lay off those sliders down and in, we'd walk a little more."

Maddon said he didn't see any anxiety in his team, but Bryant said the key to staying in this series is to relax and play as the had all season.

"Just go out there and play," he said. "Go out there and play with our heads on fire. What do we got to lose? We have to win three of them. When we're playing the best, it's when we're smiling and having fun, goofing around. Hopefully we'll see some more smiles out there, just enjoy ourselves.

"It's a little bit hard to relax, the early part of the game. It's the World Series. We're all young. Everybody feels the nerves, but I think as these games keep going on, we're feeling a little more comfortable with it. Hopefully tomorrow we can continue to do that."

The Indians struck back against Lackey and the Cubs in the second. Carlos Santana led off with a home run. Third baseman Bryant made 2 throwing errors in the inning, the second led to a run as he threw the ball away on Kluber's infield bouncer.

"A couple of things didn't go my way, and they had the homer," said Lackey, who wanted the first pitch to Santana called a strike instead of a ball. "That changed the at-bat quite a bit."

A double by Jason Kipnis and a single by Francisco Lindor in the third made it 3-1 Cleveland.

The Indians got another run in the sixth and put it away in the seventh on a 3-run homer to right field by Kipnis against reliever Travis Wood. Ace reliever Andrew Miller worked 2 innings for Cleveland.

"We're just going to have to play better," Lackey said. "There's plenty of talent in this room to win a ballgame tomorrow. We've just got to execute and play a good baseball game."

For Indians manager Terry Francona, nothing changes.

"The only thing that changes is we'll pack our bags because we're going to go home or way or the other, and we'll show up and try to beat a really good pitcher tomorrow, and that's what we always do. Nothing needs to change."

At least not for one team. WS

Dexter Fowler hits a solo home run in the eighth inning. Fowler scored both of the Cubs' runs in the 7-2 loss. (Steve Lundy/Daily Herald)

WORLD SERIES » GAME 5

October 30, 2016 • Chicago, Illinois • Cubs 3, Indians 2

Raise the Flag

Cubs Find Themselves Just in Time

By Barry Rozner, dailyherald.com

Deep in slumber in San Francisco, the Cubs came out of hibernation.

Just when it was looking darkest in Los Angeles, they woke up and remembered they were the Cubs.

And Sunday night in Chicago, facing the end of the 2016 season, they found themselves.

Just in time.

With Jon Lester pitching lights-out again when they needed him most, and Aroldis Chapman recording an 8-out save, the Cubs finally came up with a little offense and held on to defeat Cleveland 3-2 in Game 5 of the World Series, the first victory at home for the Cubs in the Fall Classic since 1945.

"The story starts and ends with Jon for me," said catcher David Ross. "Personally, not a better way to go out in my last start and catching Jon Lester, who won a World Series, for me and all the things he's done for me personally.

"To be on this stage and catching Jon Lester, what a way to go out."

Lester was brilliant but trailing 1-0 in the bottom of the fourth when Kris Bryant led off with his first home run in 12 games to tie it against Trevor Bauer, and Wrigley Field was alive and buzzing for the first time in three days.

Anthony Rizzo followed with a double into the vines in the right-field well and the Cubs were in business.

Ben Zobrist ripped a 3-0 fastball to right and when Addison Russell reached on a swinging bunt, Rizzo scored to give the Cubs the lead. After a Jason Heyward strikeout and a Javy Baez bunt basehit, Ross' sacrifice fly gave the Cubs a 3-1 lead.

"The (Bryant) home run was huge, getting the crowd back in it," Ross said. "When we get the lead, we play a lot better."

The Indians threatened again in the fifth with a leadoff double, but Lester was masterful in getting out of it and the Cubs held onto their 3-1 lead.

It was the biggest inning of the World Series for Lester and the Cubs.

Willson Contreras embraces closer Aroldis Chapman, who entered during the seventh inning of Game 5. (Steve Lundy/Daily Herald)

"I was grinding quite a bit those last couple innings," Lester said. "I knew I had to make perfect pitches in a game like this."

The Indians got one back in the sixth largely due to Lester's inability to hold a runner on at first, but Ross minimized the damage when he threw out Francisco Lindor trying to steal to end the inning.

But Joe Maddon pulled Lester after 6 innings and only 90 pitches, and left it up to the bullpen, starting with Carl Edwards, who gave up a leadoff single to Mike Napoli in the seventh.

With one out and Napoli on second, Maddon went to his closer, who got out of the inning and the Cubs still led 3-2.

"With the way Jon was pitching, I didn't expect to come in that early," Chapman said through his interpreter. "But (Maddon) told me early in the day that I might be pitching in the seventh."

Chapman got the first out of the eighth and then Rizzo made a great diving stop of a Rajai Davis hit down the line, but Chapman never moved off the mound and it went for an infield hit.

Opposite: Third baseman Kris Bryant connects for a home run in the fourth to tie the score. The Cubs would take the lead later that inning on Addison Russell's RBI single. Top: Anthony Rizzo makes a diving play at first, though the Indians' Rajai Davis was still able to record an infield single. (Steve Lundy/Daily Herald)

After Davis easily stole second on Chapman, Jason Kipnis popped to left and Davis stole third. That left it up to Lindor, who took a called third strike and Chapman had survived the eighth.

At 30 pitches through 5 outs, Chapman entered the ninth needing 3 more outs to get the Cubs on a plane to Cleveland.

Napoli led off and grounded to short for the first out, Carlos Santana popped to right and Jose Ramirez—who homered in the second off Lester—struck out on Chapman's 42nd pitch and the Cubs had survived to fight another day.

That day will be Tuesday in Cleveland.

"(Chapman) threw really well tonight," Ross said. "He really pitched tonight. He threw a changeup to Napoli. He threw sliders.

"It's the World Series and everybody has to do the best they can. Their (relievers) are over there pitching multiple innings. It's nice to see (Chapman) sort of match them."

It wasn't easy, again, but the Cubs have a one-game winning streak and have forced a Game 6.

"There have been times in the postseason where we just kind of forgot who we were," said Cubs president Theo Epstein. "That happens when you're facing good teams, but we know what we have to do and we know how to get out of it and kind of find ourselves again."

They did it just in time Sunday night. **WS**

Jason Heyward snags a fly ball for an out in the third inning of Game 5. Heyward was a defensive force in right field all season despite struggling at the plate. (John Starks/Daily Herald)

> **WORLD SERIES » GAME 6**
>
> November 1, 2016 • Cleveland, Ohio • Cubs 9, Indians 3

On the Cusp of History

Cubs Force World Series Game 7 Against Indians

By Bruce Miles, dailyherald.com

The grandest words in sports: Game 7 of the World Series.

The Chicago Cubs forced the Fall Classic to its limit Tuesday night, and they did so in the grandest of fashions.

Addison Russell's grand slam in the third inning off reliever Dan Otero broke open a 3-0 game and helped lift the Cubs to a convincing 9-3 victory over the Cleveland Indians in Game 6 at Progressive Field.

The Cubs have rallied from being down three games to one in the Series and will send Kyle Hendricks to the mound Wednesday night against Indians ace Corey Kluber, who again will be pitching on three days' rest.

On the brink of elimination just Saturday, the Cubs now are a victory away from their first World Series title since 1908.

"Anybody who plays this game grows up dreaming of winning a World Series," said third baseman Kris Bryant, whose two-out solo homer in the first inning got things going as the Cubs wound up scoring 3 runs.

"We get to play in a Game 7 tomorrow. That's pretty special."

The first inning began innocently enough for Indians starting pitcher Josh Tomlin. He opened the game by getting Dexter Fowler on a lineout before retiring Kyle Schwarber on a groundout to deep second base, as the Indians had the shift on.

By then, the Indians fans in the crowd of 38,116 were in full throat. Seconds later, it was the large number of Cubs fans making all the noise as Bryant lofted a hanging curveball over the wall in left.

That was only the beginning. Anthony Rizzo singled, as did Ben Zobrist, moving Rizzo to third. Russell then lifted a fly to right-center, but center fielder Tyler Naquin and right fielder Lonnie Chisenhall got mixed up and allowed the ball to drop for a double, scoring both runners.

Russell's grand slam in the third gave him 6 RBI for the game, equaling the World Series single-game record.

Anthony Rizzo cheers as Ben Zobrist scores during the Cubs' 9-3 victory in Game 6. (John Starks/Daily Herald)

Despite some ups and downs at the plate, Russell has had some big hits, both in the National League championship series and the World Series.

"Honestly, it's been throughout the whole year," he said. "Being part of the Cubs, you're being put in the limelight. And early on you're forced to deliver when the game is on the line. So having practice throughout the whole season, and then finally here comes the big moment in the postseason, in the World Series."

The Cubs sent Jake Arrieta to the mound, and he went 5⅔ innings, giving up 3 hits and 2 runs. He walked three, struck out nine and threw 102 pitches.

"Jake was really good," manager Joe Maddon said. "On his regular rest, he was outstanding."

When Arrieta walked Chisenhall with two outs in the sixth, Maddon turned to left-hander Mike Montgomery. Montgomery got help in a nice stop by Russell at shortstop to start an inning-ending forceout at second.

Opposite: Jake Arrieta restricted the Indians to 2 runs, earning praise from manager Joe Maddon. Top: Kris Bryant opened up the Cubs' scoring in Game 6 with a first-inning solo home run. (John Starks/Daily Herald)

It was another early entry into a game by closer Aroldis Chapman, who worked 2⅔ innings to close out Game 5. On Tuesday, Maddon brought him in with two outs and two on in the seventh.

Chapman retired Francisco Lindor on a 3-1 groundout. Lindor originally was called safe, but a replay review overturned the call. Chapman had to scurry to cover first base, and he appeared to turn his ankle stepping on the bag.

While the replay review was under way, the Cubs' athletic trainer visited Chapman, who walked off the field in little apparent difficulty.

Rizzo added insurance with a 2-run homer in the ninth. Pedro Strop replaced Chapman after Brandon Guyer's leadoff walk in the bottom of the ninth.

"Seventh inning, the middle of the order was coming up," Maddon said of bringing Chapman in. "So I thought the game could have been lost right there if we did not take care of it properly.

"Also, there was the threat that we would score more runs, which we did and just did not have enough time to get (Pedro Strop) warmed up after the 2-run home run by Rizzo."

With all that has happened in this Series, Maddon said it's only fitting it's going to Game 7.

"It's been a very well-contested series," he said. "Both sides have played really good baseball. Again, of course, we want to be the group that breaks the string, but you're probably right, it's just correct and apt that we'd go seven games." **WS**

Addison Russell's third-inning grand slam tipped the odds emphatically in the Cubs favor as they worked to force a Game 7 in Cleveland. (John Starks/Daily Herald)

WORLD SERIES » GAME 7

November 2, 2016 • Cleveland, Ohio • Cubs 8, Indians 7 (10 innings)

Blue Heaven!

The Chicago Cubs are World Series Champions

By Bruce Miles, dailyherald.com

World champion Chicago Cubs.

That has a certain ring to it, doesn't it?

The Cubs earned their championship rings along with an exalted place in Chicago sports history Wednesday night with an 8-7 victory in 10 innings over the Cleveland Indians in Game 7 of the World Series at Progressive Field.

Ben Zobrist, named the MVP of the series, hit an RBI double down the left-field line to drive in pinch runner Albert Almora Jr. with the go-ahead run. Miguel Montero added an RBI single for insurance. The Cubs needed that insurance because the Indians scored a run in the bottom of the inning on an RBI single by Rajai Davis, who hurt the Cubs badly in the eighth.

The World Series victory was the first for Chicago's National League ballclub since 1908, and it forever put to rest talk of myriad curses or jinxes.

Cubs fans couldn't help but think all the forces of nature and beyond were working against them when the Indians scored 3 runs in the bottom of the eighth inning, with the final two coming on Davis' homer off closer Aroldis Chapman to tie the game at 6-6.

"The clock resets to zero now," said pitcher Jake Arrieta. "One hundred and eight years doesn't really mean anything to anybody anymore after tonight. To be a part of that to bring a championship to Chicago and just be a part of this group, it's humbling, it's rewarding and we deserve it, man."

The wildly entertaining—and sometimes sloppy—game was played before a raucous gathering of 38,104 fans, with an atmosphere resembling at times a college football rivalry game or a European soccer match, with fans of each team singing and chanting back and forth.

Before the 10th inning started, rain delayed the game 17 minutes.

"I think the rain delay was the best thing that ever happened to us, to be honest with you," said general manager Jed Hoyer. "It was a break in the game. Things had stopped going in our direction. We went down and talked a little bit. Theo (Epstein) and I saw the same

Following the final out of Game 7, the Chicago Cubs celebrate making history. (John Starks/Daily Herald)

thing. All our hitters were huddled in the weight room during the delay.

"I felt great. I walked up into the stands. I said, 'Win this inning, and we're world champions. Maybe after 108 years, you get some divine intervention, right?'"

Hoyer spoke to the meaning of the title.

"To me, it's all about getting home and enjoying it with our fans," he said. "So many generations have gone through this. That's really what it's all about. It's bigger than these 25 guys. It's about the city that stuck by the team forever. That's really what it means."

In the winning clubhouse, players chanted, "We never quit, we never quit," before opening the champagne bottles.

"This one about made me pass out," Zobrist said. "The way that the Series has been up and down, the elation of being up early … it was an epic battle."

The Cubs, winners of 103 games during the regular season, had to get out of their own way to win this one. Second baseman Javier Baez made 2 errors early, perhaps the product of being overly amped, but he atoned by hitting a booming home run to center field to lead off the Cubs' fifth inning.

Catcher David Ross, brought into the game in the bottom of the fifth inning along with pitcher Jon Lester, committed a throwing error on a little groundball. A wild pitch by Lester allowed 2 Indians runs to score on one play. Ross hit a home run, also to center, with two outs in the top of the sixth.

Kyle Schwarber, coming off knee surgery, got himself thrown out at second base trying to stretch a single into a double in the third.

Dexter Fowler can't help but leap for joy as he rounds the bases after hitting a game-opening home run. (John Starks/Daily Herald)

No matter. The Cubs chased Indians starting pitcher Corey Kluber with Baez's blast and scored a run that inning off seemingly invincible reliever Andrew Miller.

The World Series victory validates the rebuilding program set forth in the fall of 2011 by team president Theo Epstein, general manager Jed Hoyer and scouting/player-development head Jason McLeod. It also is a feather in the cap for the Ricketts family, which completed its purchase of the Cubs in the fall of 2009.

"In terms of validation, this is the goal," said a champagne-soaked team chairman Tom Ricketts. "I think our guys made the right decisions to move forward and actually put a little hardware in our trophy case, which by the way, we don't have one yet."

The Cubs got going quickly in this game as Dexter Fowler led off the game with a home run to center field. A jubilant Fowler rounded first base and then ran a few steps backward on his way around the bases.

The Indians tied the game on an RBI single by Carlos Santana in the third. The Cubs went ahead 3-1 in the fourth as Kris Bryant led off with a single to left field and Anthony Rizzo followed by getting hit by a pitch. Ben Zobrist grounded into a forceout, sending Bryant to third.

Top: At 39 years old, David Ross became the oldest player to hit a home run in a World Series Game 7. Opposite: Ben Zobrist was named World Series MVP after driving in the Cubs' go-ahead run with a 10th-inning RBI double. (John Starks/Daily Herald)

Addison Russell then lifted a flyball to short center field. The ball was caught by Davis, but Bryant was able to score, sliding under the tag at home plate. Willson Contreras made it 3-1 with a double.

The Cubs increased their lead to 5-1 in the fifth. Baez's leadoff homer chased Kluber in favor of Miller. Fowler's single was wiped out on a double-play grounder off the bat of Schwarber. But Bryant walked and took off and scored on Rizzo's single to deep right field, with Rizzo going to third on the throw.

Once again, manager Joe Maddon invited second-guessing when he pulled starting pitcher Kyle Hendricks in favor of Lester after Hendricks walked Santana with two outs.

Before the game, Maddon was asked how he might use Hendricks.

"I think you need to stay with tried and true with him," he said. "Look at the score, and look where he's at. How is he pitching? Is it relatively easy? Is he on top of his game? Is he not missing? Is he struggling or working to get outs?

"Normally with him, it's 90-100 pitches you feel really good about. Every game is separate entity, but I'll just be watching closely where he's at.

"You look at the last 3 starts and he's gone 85, 85 and 91 pitches. To expect a lot more than that at this time of the year under these circumstances would be kind of a stretch."

Jason Kipnis reached second base when Ross threw wildly to first base, putting runners on second and third. Both runners scored when Lester uncorked a wild pitch, as Ross had trouble retrieving the ball.

Like Baez before him, Ross atoned with a home run with one out in the sixth. **WS**

Opposite: Anthony Rizzo takes third base on Ben Zobrist's crucial 10th-inning hit. Top: Kris Bryant is safe at home in the fourth inning on a shallow sacrifice fly by Addison Russell. (John Starks/Daily Herald)

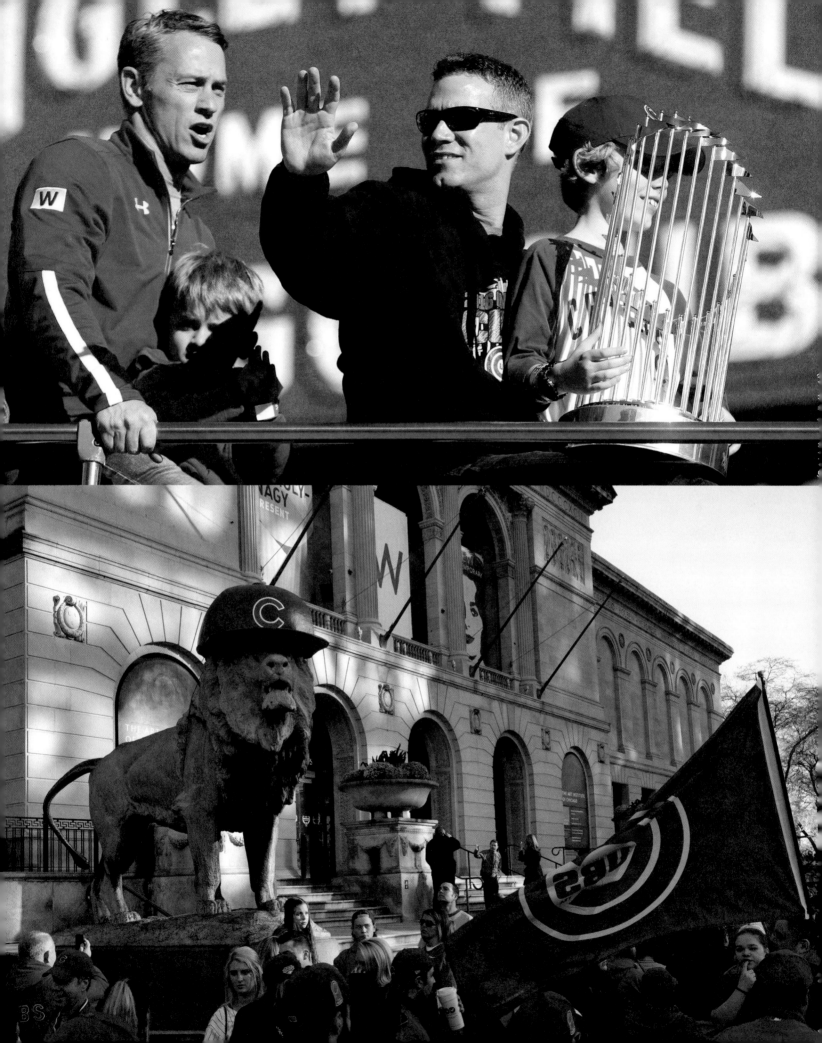

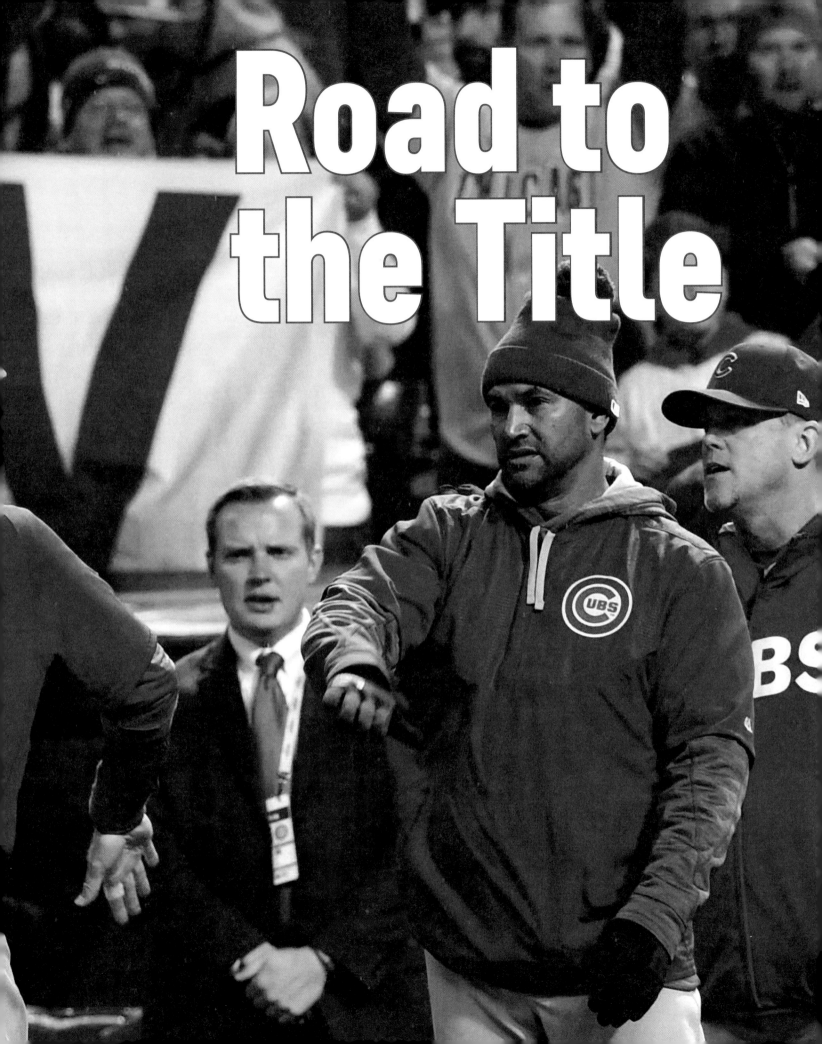

Road to the Title

Team-First Talent

Cubs' Clubhouse Not Lacking in Leaders

Bruce Miles, dailyherald.com | May 21, 2016

Walk into the Chicago Cubs' sparkling new clubhouse and the first thing you notice is the shape: a perfect circle.

The diameter of that circle is 60 feet, 6 inches, meaning pitcher Jake Arrieta could warm up with catcher David Ross from across the room. The circle also means that no one locker is any more important than any other — neither status nor seniority gets rewarded with a prime slice of clubhouse real estate.

One thing you won't see on the crisp white uniforms hanging in those lockers is the letter "C" emblazoned on the front of any jersey to signify a team captain.

But what you will find are team leaders at any point along that circle: Arrieta as the ace of the pitching staff and example setter through his strenuous fitness regimen; Ross as the veteran vocal leader; Anthony Rizzo as the emerging young leader; Jon Lester as the veteran pitcher who now seems more comfortable in his own skin; and John Lackey as the guy who has helped Lester relax and brought a prickly presence to a young ballclub.

Each in his own way is a leader and a team captain without need of a letter to prove it. That's the way manager Joe Maddon likes it.

"I think it's an organic situation," said Maddon, who sprinkles the word "organic" liberally into his conversations. "Leadership is taken. You can't give leadership. You can't give it to somebody. People have to take leadership. It's just the way it happens.

"You just can't anoint a leader. You can maybe through politics by having people vote for you, I guess. I've often thought that's a fabricated way of anointing a leader sometimes.

"But when you're within a group setting like this, with us there's no real hierarchy set up specifically. So if somebody wants to emerge as the leader, they have to take that. Players have to want to follow this particular person. I just can't say, 'Go put a C on your chest and all of a sudden people are going to listen to you.'"

Jake Arrieta and Anthony Rizzo have emerged as central figures in the Cubs' clubhouse. (John Starks/Daily Herald)

Good Players and the Right Players

It goes without saying that good sports teams have talent, and the Cubs are a good team. The really great ones, the memorable ones, ooze an intangible quality that comprises confidence and accountability with just the right touch of fun loving.

Watching the movie, "Miracle," about the 1980 U.S. hockey team that won the Olympic gold medal, one can't help but be struck by the line uttered by coach Herb Brooks, portrayed by Kurt Russell.

When told by his assistant, Craig Patrick, that he was missing some of the best players, the Brooks character replies: "I'm not looking for the best players, Craig. I'm looking for the right ones."

There are obvious differences between amateur and professional teams, but it never hurts to have the right players in addition to a lot of very good ones.

The Cubs seem to believe they have both.

"I think it's a good mix," said Ross, a 39-year-old veteran who says this is his final season as a player. "Obviously, talent is No. 1. You've got to have good talent to win in the major leagues. You just can't bring in a bunch of good guys.

"You've got to bring in guys who want to be great and have the ability to be great and want to be great for the right reasons."

Cubs team president Theo Epstein built two world-championship teams in Boston, and he has turned the Cubs into contenders after overseeing three losing seasons from 2012-14. Last year's team advanced to the National League championship series, and the current squad has come out of the gate as the best team in the major leagues.

This past off-season, Epstein and general manager Jed Hoyer brought in free agents Jason Heyward, John Lackey and Ben Zobrist.

Heyward was the marquee signing, and he immediately drew a crowd of followers among teammates during spring training for his baseball acumen. Lackey is a plain-spoken Texan who isn't afraid to ruffle feathers. And Zobrist is known as being among the most solid citizens in the game.

"The longer I do this, the more I realize character really matters, makeup really matters," Epstein said. "Obviously you need talent, but the mix you have is really important. I think we have a really great clubhouse, a lot of quality individuals, so you want to add to that and enhance it. You don't want to do anything that might compromise it in any way.

"Zobrist is one of the many guys who makes your club that much better. He really cares about his teammates, sets a great example and is someone you can sit down with and exchange ideas about baseball and life.

"He's been a great add to the clubhouse."

The edge Lackey brings also is important, according to Epstein.

"We have so many guys who are nice guys," he said. "We played hard (last year). We played intensely, but we transitioned from to a club that's in the crosshairs and has to show up every night over the course of 162 (games) to get where we want to go.

"Someone like Lackey demands excellence from his teammates. When he's on the mound, there's that little bit of extra gear. He holds everyone accountable. He's such a fierce competitor.

"It seems like a little added shot in the arm. And John's really well-liked by his teammates even though he does bring that edge every fifth day (on the mound). That's something we didn't have in quite the same way. He adds to the mix without taking anything away from it at all."

Title for a Time Gone By

The Cubs have had team captains in the past. Late Hall of Famer Ron Santo captained the club from the mid-1960s until being traded to the White Sox after the 1973 season.

The title was revived in 2000, when manager Don Baylor bestowed it on pitchers Kevin Tapani and Rick

Anthony Rizzo talks with teammates before Game 1 of the NLCS at Wrigley Field. (John Starks/Daily Herald)

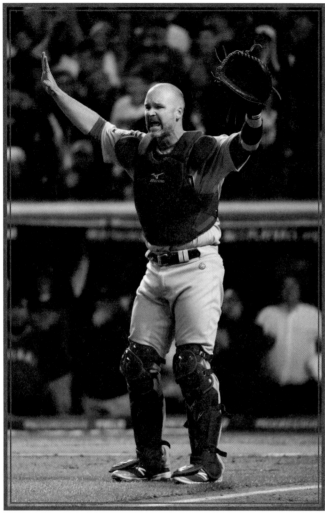

In his final season, David Ross has served a prominent role as a leader on a young Cubs team. (John Starks/Daily Herald)

Aguilera, first baseman Mark Grace and right fielder Sammy Sosa. Grace and Aguilera were gone after that season, so Baylor awarded the "C" to second baseman Eric Young and catcher Joe Girardi for 2001.

"To me, it's a responsibility," Baylor said in 2000. "It's not just thrown out there. It means something."

The modern-day Cubs don't seem to be in any rush to formalize a captain's role.

"I think that's more different teams and tradition," Ross said. "If you're looking for labels around here

to be 'the guy,' that's not the group we have in here. Everybody's 'the guy' in their own right. Everybody contributes in their own way.

"I think it's important about just knowing your role as a teammate and as a part of the club and doing your role to the best of your ability, whether that's to lead by example, to lead on the field, to lead the pitching staff, to be the second line on the pitching staff, whatever it is. Each person's role is important in its own right."

When Epstein was general manager of the Boston Red Sox, catcher Jason Varitek was the team captain. Epstein also sees no need to reprise the role with his Cubs of today.

"Personally, I don't think it's something that I ever set out to do and say, 'Hey, we should have a captain,'" he said. "If it gets to that point, it's probably too late. You probably don't have the right guys in there.

"But if somebody stands out as a clear, unquestioned leader or if somebody has been around a long time and might benefit in some way from a 'C' on his chest as a physical manifestation of what is already in place as far as a leadership dynamic, that might be something to consider. But that's not something I desire to do ever again."

As close as Maddon has come to the captain concept has been to meet with several players in spring training — players he termed "lead bulls" — to allow them to run with leadership responsibilities.

"When you are a good leader, you are really sensitive and have a lot of empathy toward everybody else around you," the manager said. "If you are looking for guys in clubhouses, I would look for empathy as much as anything regarding whether or not you believe somebody's a leader. And also listening skills and somebody who is not always pontificating. That leads you in the wrong direction.

"I like the fact that it's spread out among them. The topic was leadership. I think that has to be taken more than it's being given." **WS**

Despite being a new face on the Cubs roster this season, Ben Zobrist has played under manager Joe Maddon for much of his career and is known for his ability to lead by example. (John Starks/Daily Herald)

Smart Moves

How the Chicago Cubs Have Used Trades to Build a Contender

Bruce Miles, dailyherald.com | September 9, 2016

Being the smart young man he is, Kyle Hendricks had at least an inkling what the Chicago Cubs were doing when they traded for him in July 2012.

"When I first got traded, I was a little bit aware of it," said Hendricks, a pitcher who came over from the Texas Rangers with third baseman Christian Villanueva in a trade for pitcher Ryan Dempster. "Obviously, after I came over, I became much more aware of what the process and the plan that was put in place.

"I was one of the early parts. They've made a lot of moves since I've been here, with a lot of these young guys, especially position players. Even when I got traded, you could see the ball had definitely started rolling."

For all the talk of the Cubs' drafting prowess since team president Theo Epstein and his crew came to Chicago in the fall of 2011, trades have been just as important a factor in building an inventory of young talent.

Epstein and general manager Jed Hoyer took veteran pitching assets such as Dempster, Jeff Samardzija, Jason Hammel (whom they since reacquired), Matt Garza and Scott Feldman and turned them into young prospects such as Hendricks, pitcher Jake Arrieta, shortstop Addison Russell and relievers Pedro Strop, Carl Edwards Jr. and Justin Grimm.

They also traded young pitcher Andrew Cashner to the San Diego Padres for a first-base prospect named Anthony Rizzo.

Of the 25 active and 10 disabled-list players the Cubs had on the roster at the end of August, 17 came from trades, eight were major-league free agents, six were drafted, one (Hector Rondon) came from the Rule 5 draft and three were undrafted amateur free agents, including outfielder Jorge Soler and catcher Willson Contreras.

There were a few howls of protest when the Cubs made some of these trades. The losing seasons of 2012, 2013 and 2014 were painful to watch, but without these trades the Cubs aren't where they are today: coming

While Theo Epstein's draft choices and free-agent signings have received plenty of attention, the Cubs' president has built this historic team on a foundation of visionary trades (Steve Lundy/Daily Herald)

Anthony Rizzo (Joe Lewnard/Daily Herald)

Addison Russell (Steve Lundy/Daily Herald)

off a deep playoff run last year and poised to win a division title this season.

For the players acquired in the trades, it has been fun for them to see what has happened since the Cubs were losing a lot more than they were winning.

Grimm came to the Cubs with Edwards, third baseman Mike Olt and reliever Neil Ramirez in a July 2013 trade with Texas for Garza.

"When I first got traded, I would say I had no clue," Grimm said of the Cubs' plan at the time. "I just thought I was going to a different team. After being over here that September, I started to learn a lot about the organization and what they were pushing for.

"It's just been unbelievable, not only the guys they've already drafted and have already made it here but just the guys with trades that they brought over."

Although Hendricks, Grimm and Edwards all were drafted by the Rangers, they weren't teammates in the minors.

"I was in my first spring training with C.J. (Edwards)," Hendricks said. "We actually hung out a lot together. Grimm was always a level or two ahead of me in the minors, but I hung out with him in spring training.

"I had one spring training with Texas. I briefly knew them. When all of them came over, it was pretty cool."

Each, however, was aware of the talent the others possessed.

"Absolutely," Grimm said. "I would say Kyle has opened my eyes up a lot this year. He was always that smart pitcher in the minor leagues going through lineups, but it's a whole different story here going through that third and fourth time. To see him grow this year has been nothing short of impressive."

It was during a stay at Class AAA Iowa in 2013 that Hendricks first caught sight of Arrieta, who had just arrived from Baltimore with Strop in a deal that sent Feldman and catcher Steve Clevenger to the Orioles.

When the Cubs acquired Arrieta, they sent him to Iowa, brought him up for a spot start and then sent him back to Des Moines. Arrieta returned to the Cubs for good -- and then some. He went 10-5 with a 2.53 ERA in 2014 before winning the Cy Young Award last year with a record of 22-6 and an ERA of 1.77.

Hendricks remembers catching a glimpse.

"Right when I got called up to Iowa, he was there," Hendricks said. "I don't think I could have ever imagined it coming to this because I knew nothing about him. I didn't even know who he was. When I did show up in Iowa and saw him throw for his first game, I think he struggled a little bit.

"He had some walks and gave up some runs, but the one thing I noticed right away was his stuff, and we even talked about it in the locker room.

"It was the best stuff pretty much in baseball that we had seen at that point. That was always there, and I know that's probably why the Cubs were pretty high on him from the start, if he could just figure it out.

"Obviously, he puts all the hard work and dedication into it to figure it out, to let his body figure it out. His stuff is still premier, one of the best in the game, and now his mechanics are solid, and he's got that command to go with it."

Russell was one of the final big young trade pieces, coming in a July 4, 2014, firecracker of a deal with Oakland that sent Samardzija and Hammel to the A's for Russell, pitcher Dan Straily and outfielder Billy McKinney.

"After the trade, I just wanted to come here and come to a good ballclub," Russell sad. "I really didn't know what to expect.

"I thought whenever I got here, it was a great ball team. I was placed in Double-A, and they had a lot of great guys that I've gotten to know. Some of them are here in the major leagues right now. It's pretty cool. I've been blessed that the Cubs gave me the opportunity to play."

One could argue that the Cubs pulled off multiple heists in getting these young players. In fairness to the teams that traded them, those teams wanted to win immediately, and one way of doing that is by trading prospects for veterans who can help down the stretch.

But give credit to the Cubs for scouting a Cy Young winner in Arrieta, a Cy Young candidate this year in Hendricks, and a possible Gold Glove winner and future MVP in Russell.

It was just three years ago this month that Hendricks sat in the dugout at Wrigley Field for the first time and talked about being the Cubs' minor-league pitcher of the year before going on to finish work for his degree at Dartmouth.

"It seems like the blink of an eye, and I'm here where I'm at already," he said. "You always project where you're going to go or what's going to happen, but this for me is above and beyond anything I ever imagined. Even coming into this season I had goals that were much lower than where I'm at right now.

"I'm just trying to take every day, take in what I can, learn from the game, learn from my peers, the other guys we have on this staff. Just go day to day and know what my body needs and try to keep this consistency going.

"We all know what we want to accomplish in October and where this whole team is headed." **WS**

Jake Arrieta (Joe Lewnard/Daily Herald)

Kyle Hendricks (John Starks/Daily Herald)

Flashing the Leather

Defense Rules the Day for Chicago Cubs

Bruce Miles, dailyherald.com | September 22, 2016

For the Chicago Cubs, the defense never rests.

First, the defense is good, with Gold Glove candidates all across the diamond and high rankings in some of the more advanced defensive metrics.

Second, this defense is versatile, so manager Joe Maddon rarely allows it to rest.

Within the course of a single game, Kris Bryant may start at third base, move to left field and the move back to third base.

Ben Zobrist may take the second base-left field-right field route.

Javier Baez is a glove whiz at whatever infield spot Maddon puts him.

That kind of defensive versatility has been important in the regular season, and it can become even more important during the upcoming postseason.

"I'll say it again: Game in progress, to have guys like that, and I don't even have to worry, if I want to do something, 'You can do this. You can do this. You can do this,'" Maddon said. "It's in there. It's within those names.

"You can do all this crazy stuff defensively and feel good about it. A lot of teams can't. They won't put so-and-so in left field or third base or whatever, because they can't. We can.

"We talk about it, but I don't think people really understand how unique that is, that you have a variety of different young players that play a variety of positions well, where you don't lose anything on defense."

That's one key. Another is that the Cubs don't have to lose a big bat by taking someone off their first position in the field.

"I think that's the big thing," pitcher Jon Lester said. "You're not losing that spot in the order. You're not losing a bat like KB or Zo or even Javy. You can move Javy around, move Zo and KB to the infield-outfield.

"I think it makes Joe's life a lot easier. You can mix and match and do what you need to do and not have to worry about giving up that spot in the lineup."

Javier Baez's speed and positional flexibility have changed the complexion of the Cubs' defense in 2016. (Steve Lundy/Daily Herald)

The traditional stats of errors and fielding percentage don't do the Cubs' defense justice. They rank in the middle of the pack in those categories.

Even though the metrics on defense are evolving and there is widespread disagreement about how accurate some of the new stats are—such as ultimate zone rating—these Cubs pass the "eye test." They also lead the league in such new measures as defensive efficiency ratio and FanGraphs' overall defensive rating, simply called "def," or defensive runs above average.

The Cubs could have a pair of Gold Glove locks in shortstop Addison Russell and right fielder Jason Heyward. First baseman Anthony Rizzo is a strong defender, and Maddon has said he'd like to see Gold Gloves awarded for players who play more than one position.

Speaking of playing more than one position, it wouldn't work unless the players were willing to do it. For example, Bryant was drafted as a third baseman, and he's the MVP front-runner this year. But he's never said he's only a third baseman.

"It's really important," Maddon said. "It makes it all work. Without that concession on their part, it's much more difficult to ask people to do different things. To break them in at an early age to be used and be into it matters a lot, too.

"For me, for us, it's very helpful. And I think you're seeing it more. Different teams are doing different things like that.

"You see guys going all over the place right now. I think the primary consideration is, 'Can he play the defense at other spots? Is he able to?' If he's not, of course you cannot do that. But when he's able to and he accepts it, it makes your bench a lot longer. It makes the game easier to manage, in a sense."

As for the pitchers, they'll gladly reap the benefits. And they provide the ultimate eye test.

"The whole defense has been fun to watch and fun to pitch for," Lester said. "Catching and throwing the baseball, you get the outs you're supposed to get.

"Come playoff time, that makes things a lot easier. If you're throwing the ball around the baseball field or not making plays, the more baserunners you have, the harder it is for us. You give them more opportunities.

"Really in the playoffs, 1 or 2 runs makes the biggest difference in the world. If we're able to limit those situations and keep our offense within striking distance, we've got a pretty good chance." **WS**

Opposite: Shortstop Addison Russell was one of four Chicago Cubs nominated for a 2016 Gold Glove Award. Anthony Rizzo, Jason Heyward, and Jake Arrieta also received nominations. (John Starks/Daily Herald) Top: First baseman Anthony Rizzo puts the tag on Cleveland Indians third baseman Jose Ramirez during Game 3 of the World Series. (Steve Lundy/Daily Herald)

Looking Back

6 Moments That Mattered for Chicago Cubs This Season

Bruce Miles, dailyherald.com | October 4, 2016

The other day in Cincinnati, Chicago Cubs manager Joe Maddon couldn't come up with one defining moment for a 2016 club that won 103 games.

Instead, Maddon said the successful season was more of "an amalgam of work."

Maddon is probably right. From the get-go, the Cubs steamrollered over the National League Central, winning the division by 17½ games over the St. Louis Cardinals, last year's division champs.

Although there may not have been one season-defining game or series, there were many moments that mattered.

Let's take a look at a few and what they meant in the grand scheme of this grand season:

Living in a Tree

The Cubs got off to a 25-6 start, prompting comparisons with the 1984 Detroit Tigers, who began 35-5 on the way to a world championship.

The tone was set Opening Night in Anaheim, with a convincing 9-0 victory over the Angels.

"I sensed it after Opening Night in Anaheim where we played such a wonderful ballgame, an all-around game," Cubs president Theo Epstein said at the time the Cubs had their 25-6 record. "I was in the clubhouse after the game.

"I got a sense from the players there was this feeling of recognition of how well they can play when they're locked in. They were almost impressed by themselves."

At the same time, Epstein was prophetic, when he warned of tougher times ahead.

"We're thrilled with the start we've gotten off to, obviously, but we're not blinded by it," he said. "We know we're in a stretch right now where winning seems far easier than it actually is. But we know there's going to be a stretch, probably a long stretch this year, where winning even one game seems virtually impossible. It's just the nature of baseball.

"We're not blinded by it. We've been saying in the office we're in a tree. We'll stay up there as long as we can. We're going to get down at some point."

Jake Arrieta celebrates with catcher David Ross after the final out of his no-hitter against the Reds in April. (John Minchillo/AP Photo)

Another No-No

Jake Arrieta didn't have his best command on the night of April 21 at Cincinnati, but that didn't stop him from pitching his second no-hitter, a 16-0 victory over the Reds.

At the time, Arrieta's record improved to 4-0 with an ERA of 0.87.

The command issue was a harbinger of things to come, as last year's Cy Young winner battled it all season, finishing 18-8 with a 3.10 ERA. That's not at all bad, but Arrieta constantly found himself being compared with last year's Arrieta, who went 22-6 with a 1.77 ERA and a no-hitter on Aug. 30, 2015, at Los Angeles.

Oh, Contreras

With catcher-outfielder Kyle Schwarber having gone down with a season-ending knee injury in the first week of the season, the Cubs were looking for more offensive spark behind the plate.

They got a bonfire on the night of June 19, when Willson Contreras hit the first major-league pitch he saw for a home run to help the Cubs to a 10-5 victory over the Pirates.

Contreras has been a work-in-progress behind the plate, and Maddon relied more heavily on veterans David Ross and Miguel Montero down the stretch, something he's likely to do in the playoffs.

In Sunday's season finale at Cincinnati, Contreras started at catcher and moved to left field, a position he could play at times during the playoffs.

Contreras finished the season with a line of .282/.357/.488 with 12 homers and 33 RBI.

The Cubs are likely to carry three catchers in the postseason, and if they make it to the World Series, Contreras could become an attractive DH option in the American League park.

Falling Out of the Tree

As Epstein warned, the Cubs hit a rough patch from late June and into July, finishing with a 6-15 stretch into the all-star break.

Catcher Willson Contreras has vaulted from mid-season call-up to lineup staple in his 2016 rookie year, even taking on the position of left field when needed. (Joe Lewnard/Daily Herald)

In their final 10 games leading into the break, the Cubs did not get a quality start.

A victory at Pittsburgh on July 10 snapped a five-game losing streak. But things were in the works or on the way that would help in the following weeks.

It was right before the break that Maddon inserted Adam Warren (since traded to the Yankees) as a sixth starting pitcher. That gave the rotation regulars a break, as did Maddon holding Jon Lester and Arrieta back until the fourth and fifth games, respectively, when play resumed after the All-Star Game.

Then on July 25, the Cubs traded for closer Aroldis Chapman, giving them a lockdown closer.

Anthony Rizzo's MVP-caliber season helped the Cubs cross the century mark in wins. (John Starks/Daily Herald)

Maddon predicted the Cubs had another good run in them, and he was right. They came out of the break and went on a 36-14 run.

Seattle Stew

Maddon and Cubs showed a nationwide TV audience just about everything on Sunday night, July 31.

They beat the Seattle Mariners 7-6 in 12 innings, with the winning run scoring on a squeeze bunt by Lester, who came off the bench as a pinch hitter.

Also in that game, Travis Wood came in as a relief pitcher, moved to left field and came back in to pitch. He went back-first into the left-field wall to make a catch.

The Clincher and 100

On the night of Sept. 15, the Cubs lost 5-4 to the Brewers at Wrigley Field. They wound up clinching the division later that night with a Cardinals loss, so they simply moved the party to the next day.

Maddon's next goal was 100 victories, which happened Sept. 26 at Pittsburgh.

It was the franchise's first 100-plus winning season since the 1935 club won 100 and the sixth 100-plus-win season in team history.

With all of that, Maddon's challenge was—and remains until the playoffs start—to keep the team both rested and fresh.

Maddon and the Cubs have seemed up to that challenge so far. Since clinching, they went 10-5, with one rain-shortened tie game.

After a day of rest Monday, the Cubs will get back at it Tuesday with simulated-game action at Wrigley Field before Wednesday and Thursday workouts in advance of the division series opener Friday at home.

That's when the moments that really matter will begin. **WS**

Wrigley Renaissance

For Chicago Cubs' Epstein, Vision Accomplished

Bruce Miles, dailyherald.com | October 23, 2016

Four years ago to the day Sunday, Chicago Cubs president Theo Epstein met with a few of us media types.

He wanted to move past the just-concluded 101-loss season and look to the future.

"I actually walked around Wrigley the other day, this Sunday with my son, and saw the ivy was red, orange," Epstein said on Oct. 23, 2012. "I just kind of flashed to how great it would be to be playing baseball this time of year at Wrigley. That's the goal: to get there, but to get there in a way to get there year in and year out.

"You can't help but look at what the Cardinals are doing and the Giants now and teams that are able to be factors in October year in and year out. You can't but look at that and understand that's the goal.

"That's our goal."

The Cubs' ultimate goal—winning the World Series— hasn't been reached yet, but they did something monumental Saturday night by winning their first National League pennant since 1945.

They will try to win their first World Series title since 1908 beginning Tuesday night, when they open the World Series at Cleveland. The Indians have a world-championship drought of their own, dating to 1948.

On Saturday night, with the ivy turning those colors Epstein mentioned four years ago, you couldn't blame him if those hues looked a little more vivid to him.

The Cubs are appearing in their second straight postseason after getting swept in the National League championship series by the Mets last October. And they appear well on their way to achieving the goal set forth by Epstein, general manager Jed Hoyer and scouting/player-development chief Jason McLeod: building a foundation for sustained success.

Getting to, let alone winning, the World Series nowadays is difficult to do, what with expanded playoffs and the random nature of the game of baseball itself.

But the Cubs look to be in position to knock on the door every year for the foreseeable future.

Owner Tom Ricketts raises the NLCS trophy after the Cubs beat the Dodgers in six games. Ricketts has spearheaded and backed the overhaul of the Cubs under president Theo Epstein, whom he recently signed to a five-year extension. (Steve Lundy/Daily Herald)

The plan undertaken by Epstein and his crew wasn't without pain. In addition to the 101 losses in 2012, the Cubs lost 96 games in 2013 and 89 in 2014.

In those first three years, Wrigley Field was so quiet on some nights that a few of us in the press box likened it to a library.

But it was nothing but happy noise Saturday, as the 42,386 fans inside Wrigley Field and the thousands more on the streets of Chicago partied well into the wee hours.

The dark days of 2012, 2013 and 2014 seemed well in the rearview mirror.

Epstein acknowledged those days were harder on the fans than they were on him.

"It wasn't all that painful; it was probably more painful for our fans," he said above the din Saturday night. "For us, there were some trying moments, but it was fun being focused on acquiring young talent and having this in mind as a goal and pulling together in the same direction."

Rookies Willson Contreras (signed by the previous baseball regime) and Albert Almora Jr. were in the starting lineup Saturday as was key draft choice Kris

Bryant and still-young players for whom the Cubs traded, such as Anthony Rizzo, Addison Russell and winning pitcher Kyle Hendricks.

Infielder Javy Baez, drafted by the previous baseball-operations team, was a co-MVP of the NLCS.

The Epstein-led front office brought in the other co-MVP, pitcher Jon Lester, as well as veterans such as infielder-outfielder Ben Zobrist, center fielder Dexter Fowler, backup catcher David Ross and closer Aroldis Chapman.

"All the veterans took less (money) to sign here, to be part of this," Epstein said. "Our young guys, from the moment they were drafted, wanted to contribute to a club that could get to a World Series, win a World Series. They all set their egos aside, and they're getting rewarded for it."

Team chairman Tom Ricketts put his faith in Epstein and expressed gratitude that the fans kept the faith.

"The rebuild we've done the last four, five or six years, the people went through a lot, and they've all been with us," Ricketts said as he stood a few feet from Epstein. "It's really incredible." **WS**

Top: Generations of Cubs fans have been inspired by the whirlwind success of their revamped organization. Opposite: Anthony Rizzo, Kris Bryant, Addison Russell, and Javier Baez celebrate after winning the National League pennant. (Steve Lundy/Daily Herald)

National League Division Series

NATIONAL LEAGUE DIVISION SERIES » GAME 1

October 7, 2016 • Chicago, Illinois • Cubs 1, Giants 0

Starting Strong

Cubs Execute Plan Nicely in Game 1

By Barry Rozner, dailyherald.com

Count Tom Ricketts among the few who are unafraid.

Sure, he understands Cubs Nation has a natural fear of success. After all, history has been unkind to the North Siders, even after seasons in which they were clearly the best team heading into the postseason.

But the Cubs owner, much like his manager, embraces the target and is happy to be where he is right now, starting the postseason at home as the favorite to win it all.

"We have the best team in baseball," Ricketts said, "and we think we have a better chance than some teams."

Know that Ricketts does not speak with arrogance when he says it, merely confidence that his team has done all it can to get ready for the first round of the playoffs, notably tearing apart the National League during the six-month processional.

"The fact is these are short series and you have to play well," Ricketts said. "You can't have a bad week or you're done. You don't have 162 games to prove how good you are.

"You have five games and then hopefully seven games, and you have to be ready right away and bring your best game every night.

"If we do, we'll be all right."

The Cubs were ready Friday night at Wrigley Field for Game 1 of the NLDS, playing great defense in support of starter Jon Lester, who battled the Giants' Johnny Cueto to a scoreless tie into the bottom of the eighth.

That's when Javy Baez jumped on a 3-2 pitch with one out in the eighth and with a mighty swing pounded a high shot through a fierce wind that had just enough to reach the basket in left.

"Shows you how big this ballpark can play," said Cubs manager Joe Maddon. "Javy absolutely crushed that ball."

A seriously pumped-up Aroldis Chapman threw a scoreless ninth and the Cubs had a crucial Game 1 victory, riding a single swing from Baez.

Cubs pitcher Jon Lester lived up to expectations in Game 1 of the NLDS, keeping the San Francisco Giants scoreless. (Steve Lundy/Daily Herald)

"I was thinking of bunting," Baez said. "Just trying to get on base."

It's easy to project confidence and even easier to talk about it, but confidence can disappear as quickly as an opposition blast onto Waveland—and for as many reasons as there were fans milling around outside the park late Friday night after the Cubs' 1-0 victory.

So the Cubs' 103 regular-season victories were good for bravado heading into their NLDS with the Giants—and little else. A bad start from Lester—the $155-million man brought here not just to start Game 1 of the postseason, but also to win it—and the Cubs would have been reeling just that fast.

With Madison Bumgarner slated for Game 3 on four days' rest Monday night in San Francisco, facing a Jake Arrieta that has struggled with command for

months, the Cubs could not risk heading to the West Coast having split the first two at home.

But you can't win two until you win the first one, and the Cubs got that done Friday night, thanks mostly to a brilliant Lester performance, some great defense and one long fly.

"Both sides really played an equal kind of a game," Maddon said. "Lester was outstanding. Cueto was outstanding. Defense was great on both sides.

"Classic kind of an old-school baseball game. Give both sides credit. It was really a well-played baseball game."

What's that we said before the series started? Pitch well and run into a home run once in a while. In October, it's not a bad way to go.

Friday night, it was the perfect way to go. **WS**

Opposite: Javier Baez's eighth-inning home run was the difference-maker in the Cubs' 1-0 Game 1 win. (John Starks/Daily Herald) Top: Joe Maddon congratulates Aroldis Chapman, who earned the save with a scoreless ninth inning. (Steve Lundy/Daily Herald)

NATIONAL LEAGUE DIVISION SERIES » GAME 2

October 8, 2016 • Chicago, Illinois • Cubs 5, Giants 2

Bullpen Gem

Cubs Take Commanding 2-0 Lead in NLDS

By Bruce Miles, dailyherald.com

The Cubs and their fans wound up breathing quite easily in the end.

Hendricks was OK. X-rays revealed only a bruised right forearm. And the Cubs came away with a 5-2 victory over the San Francisco Giants to take a commanding two-games-to-none lead in the best-of-five National League division series.

Hendricks, the major leagues' ERA champion, lasted 3⅔ innings, but he helped himself with the bat, as did his successor. Hendricks hit a looping 2-run single in the Cubs' 3-run second, when they took a 4-0 lead against former Cubs pitcher Jeff Samardzija.

Angel Pagan's liner hit Hendricks with two outs in the fourth. Manager Joe Maddon and the team's athletic trainer came out to visit Hendricks, who took a few warmup tosses. However, Maddon and the trainer decided Hendricks could go no longer, so they turned to left-hander Travis Wood.

"He's fine," Maddon said. "In that particular moment, a guy gets hit in the arm and then he throws that first (warmup) pitch and really yanks it, so I was concerned when I saw that. My message to him was, 'OK, even if you could finish this inning, more than likely you're going to go in, sit down and it's going to swell up. You got to get ice on it. You're probably not going out the next inning anyhow."

Hendricks seemed to understand.

"It feels all right now," he said. "In the moment, I didn't really feel it at the time, but once I tried to throw a couple pitches there, Joe and I were kind of having a discussion. He told me if there's anything at all, he didn't want me in there. And my fastball kind of coming out of my hand at the end just didn't really have a feel at the time."

Wood, a workhorse all year, struck out Conor Gillaspie to end the inning. In the bottom of the fourth, Wood hit a one-out home run to put the Cubs up 5-2. It was the third postseason home run by a Cubs pitcher. Rick Sutcliffe homered against the Padres in 1984, and Kerry Wood hit one against the Marlins in 2003.

"It was a special moment for me personally," said Wood, a good hitter and all-around athlete. "But just

Travis Wood was an unexpected Game 2 hero for the Cubs, pitching in relief of starter Kyle Hendricks and also hitting a home run. (John Starks/Daily Herald)

to be able to pull off the win ... was huge. (It) just feels good to be able to contribute at the plate as well as on the mound."

Wood (1-0) did his job on the mound, as well. He worked 1⅓ scoreless innings to start a five-pitcher parade out of the bullpen that culminated with Aroldis Chapman earning his second save in two nights.

The Cubs were looking forward to Hendricks' start. The 26-year-old right-hander earned the No. 2 spot in the playoff rotation, based largely on his 2.13 season ERA and his home record of 9-2 with a 1.32 ERA. So it had to be a little disappointing he wasn't able to go deeply into this game.

"It was definitely disappointing in a way," he said. "But you can't look at it like that. The situation happened like it did. I had to come out, and that's what we have done all year, is relied on everyone on this team. Everyone gets it done. Putting all those zeros up was huge. Putting on that extra run from (Wood) was huge. That's what the game was all about, really."

The Cubs wasted little time jumping on Samardzija. Dexter Fowler led off the bottom of the first with a double. Two outs later, Ben Zobrist singled Fowler home.

In the second, Jason Heyward opened with a double. Javier Baez walked, and Willson Contreras lined a single to right, loading the bases. Hendricks dropped his 2-run single into center field. After Fowler flied out to move Contreras to third, Kris Bryant brought Contreras home with a single.

The Giants cut the Cubs' lead in half in the third. Joe Panik led off with a single. Giants manager Bruce Bochy decided to bat for Samardzija, and the move paid off as Gregor Blanco doubled to the gap in left-center to score Panik. Denard Span grounded out, sending Blanco to third. Brandon Belt's sacrifice fly made it a 4-2 game. **WS**

Kyle Hendricks' highly-anticipated start was cut short when the right-hander was hit by a ball off Angel Pagan's bat. Hendricks drove in two of the Cubs' eventual five runs before exiting in the fourth inning. (Steve Lundy/Daily Herald)

NATIONAL LEAGUE DIVISION SERIES » GAME 3

October 10, 2016 • San Francisco, California • Giants 6, Cubs 5 (13 innings)

Late-Night Loss

Giants Defeat Chicago Cubs in 13 Innings

By Bruce Miles, dailyherald.com

Chicago Cubs manager Joe Maddon used the word "exhilarated" more than once, and his team lost.

And they lost in a tough way.

In a game that started Monday night and went into Tuesday morning in the Central time zone, the Cubs lost a heartbreaking 6-5, 13-inning decision to the San Francisco Giants at AT&T Park to force a Game 4.

Back-back-doubles by Brandon Crawford and Joe Panik to begin the final inning against reliever Mike Montgomery gave the Giants the victory and some hope in the National League division series.

The Cubs led this one 3-0 in the second inning on a 3-run homer by starting pitcher Jake Arrieta, and it looked like they were on their way to celebrating a clincher.

But the lead slipped away, as the Cubs stopped hitting in the middle and latter parts of the game. The Giants scored single runs in the third and fifth innings against Arrieta, who gutted out 6 innings and outlasted Giants ace Madison Bumgarner, who labored through 5.

In the eighth, the Giants went ahead as Maddon brought closer Aroldis Chapman in to pitch with two men on and nobody out. A triple off the bat of Conor Gillaspie put the Giants up 4-3. Crawford then singled to center, giving the Giants what looked to be some insurance.

The Cubs haven't quit all year, and in the ninth, Dexter Fowler walked to lead off against Sergio Romo. Kris Bryant then showed why he's the MVP front-runner as he homered to left to tie the game.

Montgomery came on in the ninth, so he was into his fifth inning of relief when the game ended.

As Maddon walked to the interview room, he said of this game: "Beautiful."

When asked in the interview room about his team taking a punch in the gut, he responded as only he can.

"Good baseball game," he said. "That's my take-away. I think that both sides should be somewhat exhilarated. Obviously, they win, so they're going to feel a bit better about it, but there's nothing on our side to be ashamed of. I was really proud of our kids, man. How about Montgomery in the eighth there."

Aroldis Chapman walks to the dugout after being relieved during the eighth inning of Game 3 in San Francisco. The Giants avoided being swept with an extra-inning victory. (Marcio Jose Sanchez/AP Photo)

"With all the adrenaline and stuff, I knew the situation of the game, and I just wanted to help my team," he said. "It was at all costs, and I came up with it."

Of course Maddon was asked about the decision to bring in Chapman for a potential six-out save. Travis Wood gave up a single to Belt to start the inning. Maddon then brought in Hector Rondon, who walked Posey. He then went to Chapman.

"I was hoping not," Maddon said of a six-out save. "Woody pitched against Belt. I liked that. He gets a base hit, and then Ronny on Posey was a better matchup based on what's been going on lately with Chapman versus Posey. So I liked that, too.

"Now had he gotten Posey out, I would have let him pitch to (Hunter) Pence right there, but there's a threat for a bunt. There's all kind of things they could have done there. And I know it's hard to bunt a 100-miles-an-hour (fastball).

"So let's just bring (Chapman) in right there, give him a little wiggle room. He gets a strikeout (of Pence), and then you feel OK about things. Give Gillaspie credit, man … So I did not want to have to do that, but I felt we had to do it under the circumstances." WS

Bryant echoed that.

"I thought it was a great effort from everybody," he said. "You can't win them all. We'll learn from it. A lot to take from it. We're all pretty exhausted. I'm sure they're exhausted, too. A lot of thinking involved, but that's playoff baseball. It's great for the game a game like that. I think it's more motivation to come out tomorrow."

The game might have ended in the ninth if not for spectacular catch by rookie Albert Almora in right field.

With one out, Brandon Belt walked. Buster Posey hit a drive toward the line in right. Almora dived, make a spectacular catch and threw to first for a double play.

Kris Bryant celebrates with Dexter Fowler after hitting a game-tying home run in the ninth. (Marcio Jose Sanchez/AP Photo)

NATIONAL LEAGUE DIVISION SERIES » GAME 4

October 11, 2016 • San Francisco, California • Cubs 6, Giants 5

Relentless Champs

2 Games That Sum Up the 2016 Chicago Cubs

By Bruce Miles, dailyherald.com

The two games had little in common, except for how the Chicago Cubs approached them and how they finished them.

One was the regular-season finale at Cincinnati. The Cubs didn't need to win the game, having clinched the National League Central more than two weeks previous. They trailed the Reds 4-2 heading into the eighth inning and 4-3 entering the ninth.

On the radio in Cincinnati, veteran Reds voice Marty Brennaman was busy saying goodbye for the season and thanking everybody from the team owner to the floor sweeper at the Great American Ball Park.

All the while, the Cubs kept pinging away at the plate, scoring 4 runs and winning the game 7-4.

The other game had much more meaning.

Tuesday night at AT&T Park, the Cubs trailed the San Francisco Giants 5-2 entering the ninth, and they were on the brink of frittering away a two-games-to-none lead in the National League division series and coming home to face the Giants' Johnny Cueto in a decisive Game 5.

But as they did in Cincinnati, the Cubs didn't quit. A porous Giants bullpen gave them an opening, and they took it, scoring 4 runs to rally for a stunning 6-5 victory and a happy trip home to get ready for the National League championship series.

In one of the media sessions during the NLDS, right fielder Jason Heyward cited the game in Cincinnati as a measure of what the Cubs are made. In the champagne-soaked clubhouse late Tuesday night, Cubs from one end of the room to the other voiced what's become a team mantra.

"We never quit," said bench coach Dave Martinez, the right-hand man of manager Joe Maddon, who had just got done saying the same thing.

Turns out, this approach is something that took life last season, when a then-surprising Cubs team won the wild-card and the NLDS before getting swept out of the NLCS by the New York Mets.

"Here we are," said third baseman Kris Bryant, a leading MVP candidate. "Last year we kind of adopted the saying, 'Never give up.' We'd say it after every big win. Today was no different."

Javier Baez drove in the deciding run with an RBI single in the ninth, capping off a 4-run rally. (Marcio Jose Sanchez/AP Photo)

That spirit was evident in Tuesday night's ninth inning, when Bryant led off with a single against Giants reliever Derek Law. Anthony Rizzo followed with a walk against Javier Lopez. Giants manager Bruce Bochy brought in Sergio Romo to face Ben Zobrist, who doubled home Bryant and sent Rizzo to third base.

Chris Coghlan came up to pinch hit, and Bochy countered with Will Smith. Seeing that, Maddon had rookie Willson Contreras bat for Coghlan, and Contreras singled up the middle to score Rizzo and Zobrist with the tying runs.

After Heyward bunted into a forceout—accompanied by a throwing error—Bochy made another move, making the bullpen call for Hunter Strickland. Javier Baez greeted Strickland with a single up the middle to score Heyward with the eventual winning run.

The outburst arrived in breathtaking contrast to how the Cubs hit—or did not hit—earlier in the game.

Until the ninth, they had just 2 hits, a home run by David Ross in the third inning and a single by Rizzo in the fourth. Both came against Giants starter Matt Moore, who gave Cubs little else.

"We needed to string a couple good at-bats together," said team president Theo Epstein from the middle of the postgame celebration. "It was starting to come (Monday) night. We hit a few balls hard right at guys. We weren't able to come all the way back.

"Finally, after all that frustration, it was released cathartically in the ninth inning. We just exploded in the ninth. It finally came to the fore for us."

Closer Aroldis Chapman came in and struck out all three Giants he faced in the bottom of the ninth, and before you knew it, the public-address announcer was telling fans the Giants would see them next April.

This is a Giants franchise that won the World Series in 2010, 2012 and 2014. This year's bunch wasn't going down without a fight.

"To do it in the postseason, on the road and against a team that's won 10 straight elimination games, is an incredible accomplishment," Epstein said. "It's hard to finish any team in a postseason series, let alone one that has their kind of pedigree and character.

"That says a lot, for not being ourselves for eight innings, to come alive like that. That says a lot about who we are."

In the middle of the clubhouse, pitcher Jon Lester, who has firmly established himself as a team leader, weighed in on the Cubs' wherewithal to win games like this.

"I think it's just our personality, it's our group," Lester said. "Yeah, you look at our lineups and you look at our staff and everything. We have a lot of talent, but we have a lot of grinders. And I think that starts top to bottom.

"We grind. Yeah, we have some flashy guys. We guys who are MVPs and Cy Youngs and stuff like that, but when it comes down to it, we're kind of like the 9-to-5 Chicago person who goes to work every day and grinds it out. That's what we do.

"That showed tonight, just with our at-bats and the way we went about our pitching and catching. You look at Rossy flying all over the place behind the plate, blocking balls and acting like he's 25. It's awesome to see. It's just the personality of our team." **WS**

Top: Chicago Cubs players and coaches pose for a team photo, having clinched a spot in the NLCS. (Marcio Jose Sanchez/AP Photo) Opposite: Cubs players celebrate on the mound after recording the final out in Game 4. (Ben Margot/AP Photo)

The Team

SHORTSTOP

ADDISON RUSSELL

Cubs' Russell May Be Setting Himself Up for Future MVP Nod

By Jordan Bernfield | August 28, 2016

When the Cubs acquired Addison Russell in a trade for Jeff Samardzija in 2014, the story goes that before Athletics general manager Billy Beane hung up the phone with Cubs president Theo Epstein, he told him, "You just got Barry Larkin."

While Addison Russell isn't a Hall of Famer yet, the season he's putting together at age 22 lends credence to Beane's prediction.

Russell has played elite defense since the day he was promoted to the big leagues last season. His immediate defensive impact on the 2015 Cubs spurred Joe Maddon to give him the permanent shortstop job, replacing five-year veteran Starlin Castro.

Russell possesses tremendous defensive range, an excellent arm, and smooth and efficient mechanics.

After a jaw-dropping diving stop last Monday night against the Padres, Russell's grace drew a comparison to another all-time great shortstop.

"Watch his feet and how he moves his feet," Maddon said. "Derek Jeter was like that, very simple. (Russell's) feet are spectacular. That's why he's so accurate. He's incredibly athletic."

While Russell dazzled on defense last year, he only showed flashes of his potential at the plate. He displayed patience, but struggled to produce consistent results. This season, he's proving that with his elite defense may come elite offense, especially from a shortstop. Entering the weekend, Russell ranked second in baseball among shortstops with 84 RBI, and his 19 home runs were the sixth-most among defensive captains, and his OPS ranked 10th. Those numbers put

At just 22 years old, Addison Russell is already one of the most talented shortstops in baseball. (Brian Hill/Daily Herald)

him on pace to hit nearly 25 home runs and drive in 108 runs.

Not bad for a kid who's just 22.

Russell is hitting his stride and gaining confidence as a batter. After his first All-Star Game appearance in July, the talented sophomore seems poised for more future hardware. Maddon is lobbying for Russell to win a Gold Glove.

"This guy on defense is getting to the point (where) there's no one like this right now," Maddon said.

If his ascent continues at the plate, he may also become a legitimate candidate to win the National League's MVP a few years from now.

While teammates Kris Bryant and Anthony Rizzo appear on a collision course to finish first and second in Most Valuable Player voting this season, Russell's elite defense at a premium position combined with his offensive potential make him a good future bet.

"I have him pegged as an MVP," Rizzo said on the "Spiegel and Goff Show" on WSCR-AM in spring training. "I tell him every day. I have the biggest baseball crush on him since he got called up. The way he plays, the way he moves. I have him pegged to win the MVP one year for sure."

That year appears to be coming sooner than later. Russell is proving in just his second big league season he may just live up to the hype.

Maybe the Cubs do have the next Barry Larkin. **WS**

Opposite: While Addison Russell's defensive skill has always been apparent, 2016 saw him realize some of the power potential many had projected. Top: Russell tags out the Giants' Gorkys Hernandez on an attempted steal during Game 1 of the NLDS. (Steve Lundy/Daily Herald)

PITCHER

KYLE HENDRICKS

Chicago Cubs' Hendricks Might Be NL's Best Pitcher

By Jordan Bernfield | September 4, 2016

No one anticipated that Kyle Hendricks would earn his way into the discussion for the 2016 National League Cy Young award—not even Kyle himself.

"I definitely didn't see myself being a part of that," Hendricks said when asked about it after 7 scoreless innings in his last start, against the Pittsburgh Pirates. "I had my sights set a little lower."

Though Hendricks began the year as the Cubs' fifth starter, he hasn't pitched like one since April. He has been their most consistent starter, and now sits atop baseball's leaderboard in earned run average.

Hendricks' sparkling 2.09 ERA illuminates his consistent dominance this season. It's four-tenths of a run lower than every other pitcher in baseball. Hendricks has allowed 3 earned runs or fewer in 18 consecutive starts and has been particularly stellar at Wrigley Field.

With a 0.82 ERA in his last 10 games at the Friendly Confines, Hendricks has limited opponents to just 44 hits in 65⅔ innings pitched, all while throwing fastballs under 90 mph.

"Put the radar gun in your back pocket and look at what he's doing," Cubs manager Joe Maddon said. "There has to be strong consideration (for the Cy Young)."

Hendricks doesn't look or act like a dominant major-league pitcher. Unlike closer Aroldis Chapman, who puts on a show with blazing fastballs at triple-digit speeds, Hendricks challenges batters with location and movement. It's a nuanced approach with a low margin for error, yet it's not as sexy.

Although he began the year as the Cubs' fifth starter, Kyle Hendricks finished the regular season with the lowest ERA in baseball. (John Starks/Daily Herald)

That's why some baseball observers can't admit Hendricks' performance is worthy of serious Cy Young consideration. Typically, pitching dominance is associated with velocity, not savvy.

Hendricks has an unassuming yet affable personality. If you saw him on the street, you might guess he was an elementary-school teacher in Lakeview.

But he studies video of opposing hitters like a professor. He formulates game plans to keep hitters off balance by changing speeds and avoiding hard contact.

According to FanGraphs, Hendricks produces soft contact 26.1 percent of the time, the highest rate in baseball. His changeup is rated the most effective in the sport this year.

If the season ended today, Hendricks would compete with the Giants' Madison Bumgarner, the Mets' Noah Syndergaard, the Marlins' Jose Fernandez, the Nationals' Max Scherzer and teammates Jake Arrieta and Jon Lester for the Cy Young Award.

Hendricks has a higher WAR than both his teammates and a better FIP. His ERA is nearly a half-run lower than Syndergaard's, seven-tenths of a run lower than Fernandez's, and eight-tenths of a run lower than Scherzer's. He has a lower WHIP (0.98) than all but Scherzer (0.91).

His numbers say he has been one of the National League's best pitchers, even if the radar gun doesn't.

"To be up there, I'm just taking it in stride," Hendricks said. "But in order to stay there, I have to keep doing the things I've been doing. Consistency and keeping a simple mindset."

With a strong September, voters may have to change up the way they view dominance. Hendricks might just be the National League's best pitcher. **WS**

Rather than overpowering batters with high velocity, Kyle Hendricks has relied on the quality and location of his pitches. (John Starks/Daily Herald)

70

MANAGER

JOE MADDON

What Makes Cubs Manager Joe Maddon So Good?

By Bruce Miles, dailyherald.com | October 7, 2016

If there is someone who can speak with authority about Chicago Cubs manager Joe Maddon, it's Ben Zobrist.

The second baseman-outfielder played under Maddon at Tampa Bay from 2006-14 before rejoining his old boss this year.

Maddon has gone through two wildly successful regular seasons with the Cubs. He came aboard in November 2014 as a complete culture changer. Armed with sayings, slogans, counterintuitive thinking and a wealth of baseball experience, Maddon took Chicago and his players by storm.

The big question I had as this season wore on was whether Maddon has changed, evolved or introduced new courses to the curriculum. In other words, is there a Maddon 2.0?

"I feel like I never left him, to be honest," Zobrist said. "It didn't feel like I had much of a period in between where he wasn't my manager.

"It's more like the times I was managed by Bob Melvin (Oakland) and Ned (Yost, Kansas City) were very short periods of time compared to the times I spent with Joe. If there's one manager that kind of feels normal to me, it's Joe.

"He hasn't changed. He's the same guy. There's a level of consistency there. He's a nonconformist by nature.

"As far as being consistent within that nonconformity, you kind of know that he's going to come up with something new every year. You know he's going to come up with different slogans. You know

Joe Maddon chats before NLCS Game 6 against the Los Angeles Dodgers. (Steve Lundy/Daily Herald)

he's going to have a philosophical approach to the season.

"Coming in and experiencing that this year was like more of the same for me. It was just with a different team."

The look and feel around the ballclub are pretty much what they were last year.

The atmosphere is loose. Formal batting practice happens with less frequency as the season moves along, as Maddon trusts his players to get work in as they see it.

Maddon still uses his pet sayings: "Never let the pressure exceed the pleasure," "A mind once stretched has a hard time going back to its original form" and "The process is fearless."

If anything has changed from 2014 to 2015, Maddon says those changes are slight.

"There's little nuances within the game, maybe teachable moments," he said. "What I really try to do is have the coaches bring the message to the players so there's a teaching point. If I absolutely feel like I have to bring it to the player, I will.

"But I really like when guys stay within their departments. I like to empower coaches. So if there's a message to be taken, I always think it's better to be coming from the coach to the player, and the player normally receives that better or well."

The players echo that.

"I feel like Joe stayed very, very consistent in his message," said veteran catcher David Ross, who will retire after the postseason. "Even from last year, I think the more you grow, the more the expectations come. The message changes only with the expectations.

"I feel like that's it. Stay true to who you are. He stayed true to who he is. I think there's more expected out of the group, and he knows the group better.

"So you may see some different things at times, but I feel like he does a good job of getting to know the players and what they can do and what he expects of them and is able to implement that during a game. But for me Joe's been as consistent as it gets."

That seems to help when Maddon makes in-game changes and has players moving from position to position and even back again. The players know ahead of time they may be used like that.

"I think that goes back to Joe," said pitcher Jon Lester. "Joe's done a good job of communicating. I think that's what makes him such a good manager. He communicates. He pulls guys aside. He talks to them as a man. I think that's a big thing.

"In this game, there are so many people who beat around the bush and not necessarily lie to you but may not tell you the complete and honest truth of why they're doing things.

"Joe has never done that. He's upfront with all our guys. I think that makes guys want to play for him no matter where they're at in the lineup or where they're at in the field."

With as loose as Maddon makes things, that doesn't mean the players are running the show, even though they have a wide berth.

Near the end of the season, after the Cubs had clinched the National League Central, pitcher Jake Arrieta briefly expressed displeasure after the Cubs changed catchers in the middle of the game. Maddon countered by saying the team had been winning in the final weeks of the season.

"He's in charge, but he doesn't put the hammer down," Zobrist said. "There's only one time I can remember being managed by him that he yelled down the dugout. Every other time he yells, he's yelling at the umpires.

"He very rarely tries to light a fire under us because he believes in the professionalism of the player, and it's your job to be prepared yourself. And he wants to put you in a position to do what you know already how to do. So he shouldn't have to tell you how to do it."

The other important thing Maddon has done is remain relevant. At 62, he's old enough to be some players' father and others' grandfather. Still, he relates. And being relevant, he says, keeps him in a job.

"I'm over 50 by several years, but I so identify with what they're doing and how they do it," he said of the players. "The one thing I always wanted to do is remain

Joe Maddon's philosophical perspective and focus on camaraderie has made him popular with players past and present. (Steve Lundy/Daily Herald)

contemporary. I think if you remain contemporary, you remain employable.

"The group that chooses to not remain contemporary only because they have to be locked in to old beliefs, at some point you become unemployable.

"Jimmie Reese, who I worked with with the Angels and lived to be (92) years old and was Babe Ruth's roommate at one point, Jimmie was the best. I always thought when I worked with Jimmie in the '80s—he passed away in the early '90s—'Here is a 90-something-year-old man who is so contemporary.' And that's why he's pertinent among these young players.

"We all think we're right all the time. We think the way we do things is right all the time. Sometimes you don't see everybody else's take on things. That's the mistake.

"Actually I may not like some of the music. That's OK. Methods of dress, I'm in. I'm good. Cars, I'm totally in.

"I just think if you permit yourself an openness to be absorbed in what's going on, then you can. If you want to fight that for some strange reason, which a lot of people do, then at some point you deem yourself unemployable." **WS**

24

CENTER FIELDER

DEXTER FOWLER

Fowler Sets Tone for Cubs in First At-Bat

By Mike Imrem, dailyherald.com | October 9, 2016

No baseball game should be over after nine pitches.

But Game 2 of the NL Division Series between the Giants and Cubs was. Essentially, anyway.

Maybe the entire best-of-five series is over, too. Again, essentially.

This game was like "Born to Run" being over after "In the day we sweat it out on the ..."

Dexter Fowler made those first nine pitches sing Saturday night and the Cubs proceeded to hum past the Giants 5-2.

The Cubs lead the series 2-0 as the teams move to San Francisco for Game 3 on Monday night.

Fowler just might end that game early as the Cubs leadoff man in the first inning.

It's what Fowler does and what he has done often for the Cubs this season and last: establish the game's tempo with his first at-bat.

Cubs manager Joe Maddon wasn't kidding last year when he started telling Fowler, "You go, we go."

In other words, how Fowler goes at the top of the batting order is how the rest of the Cubs lineup will go.

OK, so it's an exaggeration to say that Game 2 was over after nine pitches. One batter does not a victory make, right?

Still to come was Cubs starter Kyle Hendricks leaving early after being hit by a line drive; reliever Travis Wood hitting a home run; the Giants threatening but never, you know, really threatening.

Yet sometimes one batter and nine pitches can set the pace for the rest of the race.

After making a surprise return to the Cubs during Spring Training, Fowler cemented his essential presence at the top of the batting order. (Steve Lundy/Daily Herald)

On Sept. 1, Fowler fashioned a 13-pitch plate appearance that resulted in a walk from Jeff Samardzija.

The Giants' starting pitcher wound up throwing 47 pitches in that one inning and had to leave after the fourth.

On this night, those nine pitches to Fowler led to 20 in the inning, a Cubs run and a hint of what was to come.

"I thought we had him struck out," Giants manager Bruce Bochy said of the fourth pitch.

No such luck for the Giants. Samardzija was never the same and he left after the Cubs scored three more runs in the second.

"I think it's fair to say that he was a little bit off tonight," Bochy said.

By the time Samardzija departed, Springsteen would have gotten around to "… streets of a runaway American dream."

Fowler must drive opposing pitchers wacky as he drives their pitch count up.

He fouls off a strike, takes a ball, fouls off a couple more, on and on until the pitcher has no idea what to throw next.

The at-bat might result in a walk as on Sept. 1. Or Fowler might quit fooling around and rip a base hit somewhere.

This time it was the latter as Fowler doubled off the ivy in right-center field and scored on Ben Zobrist's two-out single.

Every time Fowler does something like that, it's easy to flash back to the day in spring training when the Cubs' future became as bright as the Arizona sun.

Fowler was leaving after one season. He was signing with the Orioles. The Cubs would have to adjust.

With you go-we go gone, Jason Heyward would have to move from his beloved right field to center. Maddon would have to find a new leadoff hitter.

Then, like out of a puff of smoke in a magic trick, Fowler appeared in Cubs camp and seven months later Samardzija's first nine pitches spelled doom for him and gloom for the Giants.

Dexter Fowler went 0-3 the rest of the night but that first at-bat did enough damage.

Essentially, that is. **WS**

Top: Dexter Fowler dives to deny Dodgers third baseman Justin Turner a hit. Opposite: Fowler sacrificed his belt to make a sliding catch during the NLCS. (John Starks/Daily Herald)

CATCHER

DAVID ROSS

David Ross Can't Explain Why Cubs Fans Love Him

By Barry Rozner, dailyherald.com | October 13, 2016

David Ross is not from Chicago.

He's not from Indiana or Wisconsin or anywhere in the Midwest, which can often get you an adoption label from the friendlies.

He hadn't played around these parts before, not on either side of town, before arriving as Jon Lester's caddie.

He has no ties to the Cubs in any way. He has no connection to the greatest losing streak in the history of sports.

He's played in Los Angeles, Pittsburgh, San Diego, Cincinnati, Boston, Atlanta, Boston again and finally the Cubs.

Ross will volunteer that he has never been a player of all-star contribution anywhere he has played, though others will remind that he's always been a terrific

caller of games and pitchers frequently requested his presence behind the plate.

But if you look up journeyman in the dictionary, you'll see a portrait strongly resembling David Ross.

So why, for the love of George Mitterwald and all that's holy, is Ross so beloved by a fan base that didn't know who he was two years ago?

"I have absolutely no idea," Ross said with a huge laugh when I asked him a few days ago. "I don't know. I don't know where it comes from.

"I think people respect hard work and good guys. I try to treat people the way I want to be treated. I hope people see that."

Ross is far from the most talented player on the roster, but Chicago has a natural affinity for the

Even in his final season, David Ross has continued to improve elements of his game, including his skill at picking off baserunners. (Steve Lundy/Daily Herald)

underdog. So when Ross does well, he gets a little extra from the faithful.

"Go out and play hard and do the best you can," Ross said. "That's life, right? Just trying to do the best you can every day. Work hard and see what happens."

It doesn't hurt Ross that the team's best young players continually speak publicly about his influence on them, and his importance.

"It's hard to put into words how crucial he is to everything we do, because you can't see what he does every day," Kris Bryant said. "But he's so important to this team in so many ways.

"The way he handles the staff and the catchers, and the way he helps with all the young players in this locker room. He knows so much about the game, the little things, and he shares that wisdom and that matters a lot.

"We all root for him, and we want him to do well, and when he does, it's so much fun for us."

For a 39-year-old catcher playing well in his final year, perhaps that has been the most fulfilling part of a dream season.

"When those guys say those things, it really takes my breath away," Ross said. "You're just part of a team, trying to help in any way you can. It's amazing the way they've embraced me.

"They treat me with respect, and they don't have to. They listen to me, and they don't have to. It speaks to the kind of character they have that they seek information and want to learn.

"It's just a big family in there and I love them to death."

As well as Ross has played this season, many have wondered if he would really give it up, but Ross has a big family at home and he believes it's time to share the duties with his spouse.

"Something crazy would have to happen for me to come back," said Ross, who could probably have his pick of jobs with Theo Epstein if he wanted to play, coach, manage, broadcast or just hang around. "It's more family-based.

"I got a chance to go home a couple times and see my son play one baseball game. It was really cool. My

David Ross has become a beloved figure among teammates and Cubs fans alike for his leadership presence, attitude, and work ethic. (Steve Lundy/Daily Herald)

Ross is fired up after making a successful play during the NLDS. (John Starks/Daily Herald)

daughter's getting into volleyball. I got a 1-year-old. I got my wife at home with two kids in school and one that's just started to walk. So she's ready for me to be home.

"And I kind of feel like I've lived my dream. I got to live this lifestyle for way longer than I ever thought or deserved to live it, and I've gotten to do a lot of fun things and been very successful for the skill set I have and what I bring to the table.

"At some point, if being a father and a husband is important to you, and you want to influence your kids and teach them right from wrong, it's hard to be gone for six, seven months and commit your life to baseball.

"But I'm so focused on this team and winning right now that it's hard to even go there. I really want to just enjoy this postseason."

In a season filled with cute stories, Ross wins in most categories. But there's no one, least of all Ross, who can explain why he has received so many standing ovations from the crazed population of Wrigley Field.

They don't, after all, do it for everyone, and they certainly don't do it with such frequency and at such unexpected times.

"It's really shocking sometimes," Ross said. "But I'm so appreciative. I almost cried in the box a few times late in the year. I couldn't focus.

"It's been overwhelming. I'll remember this stuff forever. For a guy like me in my last year, it's just the best. I can't thank the fans enough and I'm just so grateful to them."

There is much evidence to suggest the feeling is mutual. **WS**

34

PITCHER

JON LESTER

Chicago Cubs' Lester Finds His Comfort Zone

By Bruce Miles, dailyherald.com | October 15, 2016

To see Jon Lester now with the Cubs is to see a different guy from when he first got here.

At the end of his second season in Chicago, Lester is more willing to reveal a little more of his personality and yes, even a sense of humor. The other day in San Francisco, he was asked about being on Twitter.

"I hate it," he said with a smile before adding that he tweets in support of his charitable foundation.

He also was asked about being mistaken on Twitter for presidential debate moderator Lester Holt and whether he had met Holt. "I have not, no," he said. "I don't do anything with politics. I'm not on that."

Lester has turned out to be everything the Cubs hoped he would be when they signed him to a six-year, $155 million contract in December 2014. After going 11-12 with a 3.34 ERA last season, he had Cy Young-caliber year this season, going 19-5 with a 2.44 ERA.

He started and won Game 1 of this year's National League division series against the San Francisco Giants, and on Saturday night, he gets the assignment of pitching against the Los Angeles Dodgers' Kenta Maeda in the opener of the championship series at Wrigley Field.

Lester says his increased comfort level has been a gradual process.

A shoulder ailment in his first spring training with the Cubs set him back physically, and he admitted to trying to put too much symbolic weight on his shoulders for much of last season.

But by the time the Cubs reached last year's NLCS against the New York Mets, Lester has loosened up quite a bit.

Jon Lester has emerged as a steady, dominant force at the top of the Cubs' starting rotation. (John Starks/Daily Herald)

"I think it's a gradual process," he said Friday before the Cubs and Dodgers worked out. "You get thrown into a city with all these—I talk about expectations—expectations on your back.

"You want to live up to those, not only as a player and as a teammate and somebody that's involved in the city and the community.

"There's a lot of things last year, man: getting settled in a new place, figuring out what's going on here, the travel, the teams, all that stuff. Obviously, your teammates are first and foremost, getting to know them.

"So, yeah, you spend a full year together and you grind through that season and you make the playoffs and you come back this spring and we had two new guys come in, three new guys, one that I already knew (pitcher John Lackey).

"You're obviously going to feel more comfortable that second year as opposed to just getting thrown in that first year with a whole new atmosphere in front of you."

Behind the plate for Lester's start, as always, will be veteran catcher David Ross, who caught Lester when both were in Boston and who has had the role of Lester's personal catcher in Chicago.

Ross has noticed Lester's growing comfort level.

"I think there's a lot that goes into that with a second year around, having a successful season, not battling through the stuff he had going on in spring training last year and never really finding his rhythm until the second half and really wasn't as good as he could have been," Ross said.

"This year, building on spring training and going all the way through, he's way more comfortable, being more comfortable with the guys.

"The expectations of the contract is more over with. We've got Lackey in here, who is good for him. Yeah, he's definitely more comfortable, but there's a lot that goes into that."

When the Cubs signed Lester, they said they were getting a pitcher who could not only win, but lead other pitchers by example.

Manager Joe Maddon cited Lester pitching 8 innings in Game 1 of the NLDS to outduel the Giants' Johnny Cueto.

"That was a spectacular game, and he was able to go 8 and do what he did," Maddon said. "Having this experience definitely matters, especially as a starting pitcher. He's going to walk out there, he's going to be very comfortable in that moment, actually, inspired by that, I believe.

"Watched him the last game against the Giants, really calm demeanor. Threw the ball where he wanted to, him and David always worked well together.

"And I think, I want to believe, that the rest of the group grasped a little bit of courage from that fearless nature that he demonstrates as a starting pitcher in the playoffs.

"So all of that's there. And I witnessed it from the other side, too, when he was with the Red Sox. He's good. And right now he's at the top of his game." WS

Opposite: Jon Lester stepped into the role of Cubs ace during 2016. Top: Despite well-documented struggles on defense, Lester makes a successful fielding play during the NLDS. (John Starks/Daily Herald)

INFIELDER

JAVIER BAEZ

Javier Baez Makes Himself a Mainstay in Cubs' Postseason Lineup

By Bruce Miles, dailyherald.com | October 18, 2016

On a sleepy Saturday morning a couple of months back, Chicago Cubs manager Joe Maddon seemed taken aback by a question about Javier Baez during his pregame media briefing.

"Just a day off for Javy?" a media member asked.

Maddon's response was to ask the inquisitor if he was assuming Baez was an everyday player.

"I do remember that," Maddon said with a chuckle the other day. "Can't get him out now."

No, there is no way to take Javier Baez out of the Cubs' postseason lineup now. And there's no way to take the infectious baseball enthusiasm out of Javier Baez.

The 23-year-old infielder has turned October into his own national coming-out party. Baez has been the Cubs' best and most exciting player in the postseason, and maybe the best and most exciting in all of baseball.

He is 9-for-23 (.391) with a homer and 2 doubles combined in the National League division and championship series. He also has made one dazzling or heady defensive play after another, just as he did during the regular season.

And as the Cubs go deeper into the postseason, the media crowds around Baez before and after games grow deeper.

Baez seems to enjoy it.

"Yeah, sure, I love it," he said after Sunday night's 1-0 loss to the Los Angeles Dodgers, a game that tied the NLCS at one game apiece. "I'm pretty sure everybody here wants to be loved by the fans and the people of Chicago. I just do my job."

Baez, who was born in Puerto Rico and played high school baseball in Jacksonville, Florida, is completing

Javier Baez has transformed from a talented and versatile bench player into an essential everyday lineup presence. (Steve Lundy/Daily Herald)

his first full major-league season. He was drafted in the first round in 2011 by the previous Cubs regime, but the current group seemed to know it had something special.

"I actually went to see him in Puerto Rico when I first got the job," Maddon said. "And I was really impressed. I remember him making some really good plays at second base, and I saw him make some very good base running maneuvers.

"The issue at the time was just his hitting and long swing and all the different things, the high legs, the really extravagant wrapping of the bat.

"But he's really toned a lot of that down. But, honestly, not this but last spring training I said we're a better team with him on the field. Of course, he wasn't quite ready for all of that, but now he is."

And how.

During the regular season, Baez had a line of .273/.314/.423 with 14 homers and 59 RBI. He has played stellar defense, particularly with getting tags down quickly.

He also has demonstrated heads-up baserunning, both during the season and in the playoffs, whether it's reading the play and taking the extra base or stealing home on an attempted squeeze play.

So my question to Maddon: Can what Baez has be taught, or do players simply have it?

"It's almost impossible to teach what he's got. It really is," Maddon said. "When you get (young athletes), you know right away whether they have instincts for the game or not. You do.

"The guys that don't, what I used to attempt to do was attempt to set up game situations in practice and go through game situation, game speed, in practice and have them react and give them some kind of tangible keys to be aware of, because they don't think that way. They don't have that chip.

"The guys that lack it, you try to get them through practice and setting up situations," Maddon said. "The guys that have it, don't you dare coach it out of them."

So Maddon will do with Baez what he has said he would do all along: leave the kid alone.

"Right now I think he feels free to play," Maddon said. "I can't give him any more freedom than he's already got. He sees things. He's like a good running back; he sees the whole field. A point guard; he sees the whole court. He just sees everything. He's got that gift."

For the Cubs, it's the gift that keeps on giving. **WS**

Top: Javier Baez dives back to first base to avoid a pick-off. Opposite: Baez celebrates hitting a home run in Game 1 of the NLDS. (Steve Lundy/Daily Herald)

17

THIRD BASE

KRIS BRYANT

Chicago Cubs' Bryant Humbly Accepts Hank Aaron Award

By Bruce Miles, dailyherald.com | October 26, 2016

Kris Bryant couldn't stay too long to enjoy receiving the Hank Aaron Award.

He had something important to do: play in Game 2 of the World Series for the Chicago Cubs.

Bryant on Wednesday received the award as the top offensive player in the National League. The American League winner is David Ortiz, who recently retired from the Boston Red Sox. Ortiz was on hand at Progressive Field for the ceremony, attended by Aaron and Major League Baseball Commissioner Rob Manfred.

The ceremony took place about one hour before the World Series game between the Cubs and the Cleveland Indians.

"I want to thank all the fans and everyone who supported me for this award," said Bryant, who was allowed to make his remarks and then head back to the Cubs' clubhouse. "It's really an honor to be up here with two of the best baseball players to ever play this game. I grew up watching Big Papi (Ortiz) on the Red Sox get to this point and win a World Series, and hopefully I can do that here.

"To accept an award with one of the best baseball players ever with your (Aaron's) name on it is a true honor."

Bryant's line this year was .292/.385/.554 with 39 home runs and 102 RBI. He is a leading candidate for the National League MVP Award.

Kris Bryant more than delivered on his potential in 2016, putting up MVP-worthy batting numbers. (Steve Lundy/Daily Herald)

Ortiz just completed his career after 20 seasons. His final season was a huge one: .315/.401/.620 with 38 home runs and 127 RBI.

Ortiz paid tribute to Bryant.

"That baby boy over there at the end of the table, man," Ortiz said. "Now it's my turn to sit down and watch you doing your thing. It's so much fun watching you out there putting the team on your back. That's part of greatness. That is part of what this game is all about. I'm looking forward to many years of you playing this game."

Aaron, who spent most of his career with the Braves, said the Cubs remain a favorite of his because of the late Ernie Banks, his contemporary.

"Mr. Ernie Banks, he was an idol of mine," Aaron said. "I loved him, and I'm sure wherever he is today, he is smiling in his grave. I just want to say that I am smiling with him. I just wish that he could be here to play one more game, as he always said."

In honor of Aaron, Cubs manager Joe Maddon called Bryant "Hammerin' KB."

"It's a great achievement for him, and we're happy for him," Maddon said. "And I know he will humbly accept it in the right way."

Bryant did his best to do so.

"Yeah, it's so surreal to me," he said. "I've been through some pretty cool things recently, but this is something I'm going to have to pinch myself.

"Obviously David Ortiz had an unbelievable career, and he's going out and I'm just making my way in. Obviously one of the best baseball players that ever lived (Aaron) sitting next to me. This is such a surreal moment for me." **WS**

Top: Kris Bryant throws to first base during the NLCS. Opposite: In addition to manning third base, Bryant spent significant time in 2016 learning and playing left field to best suit the Cubs' lineup needs. (Steve Lundy/Daily Herald)

ANTHONY RIZZO

Is Rizzo Next in a Long Line of Great Chicago Athletic Leaders?

By Scot Gregor, dailyherald.com | October 28, 2016

As the assistant general manager with Boston in 2005, Jed Hoyer still remembers the Chicago White Sox arriving at Fenway Park in early October and beating the Red Sox to complete a 3-game sweep in the American League division series.

Hoyer also remembers Paul Konerko.

"You could tell he was a leader," Hoyer said. "A really solid, veteran leader."

Konerko was a guiding force for most of his 16-year hitch with the White Sox, and he helped them win the World Series in '05.

Look elsewhere around the city, and you've seen other individual engines powering their teams to championships with a combination of athletic skill and willingness to lead.

Jonathan Toews is the epitome of a leader with the Chicago Blackhawks, steering them to three Stanley Cup championships.

While winning six titles with the Chicago Bulls, Michael Jordan might have been the best leader ever in professional sports.

The Chicago Cubs have an entire clubhouse full of leaders. It's a big reason why they're in the playoffs for the second straight season and in the World Series this year.

If you're looking for an obvious go-to guy in the Cubs' clubhouse, it's natural to turn to Anthony Rizzo. An offensive force and a gifted glove at first base, Rizzo is also one of the longest-tenured players

Anthony Rizzo's performance at the plate in 2016 made him a contender for MVP alongside teammate Kris Bryant. (Steve Lundy/Daily Herald)

on this current team. Both Rizzo and relief pitcher Travis Wood have been on the roster since 2012.

But with veterans like David Ross, Jon Lester and Ben Zobrist also on the roster, Hoyer isn't ready to put the leadership spotlight completely on Rizzo.

"I think he's getting there," Hoyer said. "For now, I think David Ross has been wonderful for Anthony. I think with David there to offer that kind of guidance, three or four years from now Anthony's really going to be a leader. He just turned 27.

"As he gets older and gains more experience, I think that's going to be very important. I think Anthony wants to be a leader, and I think he's well on his way."

A good leader never panics, so Rizzo is keeping calm even with the Cubs down to the Indians 2-1 in the World Series. The Cubs also trailed the Dodgers 2-1 in the National League championship series when Rizzo was riding a 2-for-19 slump.

He got hot, and so did the Cubs.

"Personally, I was upset, but I knew the team was where we needed to be," Rizzo said. "Anything I do, anything any of us do, we want to be the best at. So it's annoying, for sure, but it's what makes our team so great is everyone has each other's back, and everyone's rooting for everyone."

Cubs outfielder Albert Almora was only 11 when the White Sox swept the Astros in the World Series, but he was paying attention to what was going on.

"I remember watching Konerko growing up, and Anthony is a lot like that," Almora said. "I never played with Paul, but Anthony, off the field, on the field, he's a definite leader. You look up to him and try to learn from him. It's great being his teammate." **WS**

Anthony Rizzo reacts to his double in the first inning of NLCS Game 6. (John Starks/Daily Herald) Top: With leadership ability to match his talent, Rizzo has become one of the faces of the Cubs franchise. (Steve Lundy/Daily Herald)

(Steve Lundy/Daily Herald)

National League Championship Series

Rise to the Occasion

Montero Grand Slam Powers Cubs to 8-4 Game 1 Win

By Bruce Miles, dailyherald.com

There's nobody in baseball who says "bring it on" to the second-guessing barroom banter quite like Chicago Cubs manager Joe Maddon. Saturday night's opener of the National League championship series will keep those second-guessers going until the egg nog runs out on Christmas Day, and that's even with the Cubs winning.

Miguel Montero hit a pinch-hit grand slam in the bottom of the eighth inning to break a 3-3 tie and lift the Cubs to an 8-4 victory over the Los Angeles Dodgers and possibly set the tone for the rest of this series.

Montero's blast came on an 0-2 pitch from Joe Blanton with two outs. Dexter Fowler immediately followed with a homer to right, and a nervous crowd of 42,376 went into party mode.

"Obviously as a kid you always dream of the situations," Montero said. "And that's what you live for. It's easy to hit a grand slam in the first inning when nobody is actually screaming at it, and this one is a lot more special because it's in front of this special crowd that we have, and you're always looking for that."

According to Elias, this was the first time in major-league history that a pinch-hit grand slam provided the game-winning run in a postseason game.

The Cubs had given up a 3-1 lead in the top of the eighth, swinging momentum the Dodgers. But the Cubs left the ballpark feeling pretty good about things in the end.

"As far as Game 1, this is a long series," said starting pitcher Jon Lester, the subject of intrigue himself. "But anytime you're able to win Game 1, that's obviously a huge boost in the clubhouse."

Now for what's sure to be a treasure trove for the second-guessers on both sides. Dodgers manager Dave Roberts walked pinch hitter Chris Coghlan intentionally with runners on first and second to get to Montero.

The Montero slam came on the heels of some moves by Maddon that might have had some Cubs fans

Miguel Montero's pinch-hit grand slam powered his team to victory in Game 1 against the Los Angeles Dodgers. (John Starks/Daily Herald)

Top: Jason Heyward slides into third base for a second-inning triple. Bottom: Ben Zobrist doubles in NLCS Game 1 at Wrigley Field. (John Starks/Daily Herald)

scratching their heads. He pulled starting pitcher Jon Lester for a pinch hitter in the bottom of the sixth in an effort to add on runs with a 3-1 lead. Lester had thrown only 77 pitches, and the move didn't pay off, as Jorge Soler grounded out to end the inning.

"I just thought that tonight, Jon wasn't really on top of his game," Maddon said. "There was a chance to put add-on runs in that particular moment."

For the second time this postseason, Maddon brought closer Aroldis Chapman in for a possible 6-out save, this time with the bases loaded and nobody out in the eighth. Chapman struck out first two batters he faced before Adrian Gonzalez lined a game-tying 2-run single to center field.

"Yeah, we had no choice," Maddon said. "I did not want to do that again. He strikes out the first two guys and then Adrian has a great at-bat. So what are you going to do about it? You just got to move on. But give

Chappy credit for keeping it at 2 (runs). Now, there's the argumentative part where we did not lose the lead."

There were several big moments for the Cubs in this game, in the field and on the basepaths.

They came out flying, as Fowler led off the bottom of the first against Kenta Maeda with a single. He scored on Kris Bryant's double to left.

The Cubs continued their good work in the second inning. Jason Heyward lined a leadoff triple to the right-field corner to start the inning.

Javier Baez, who has stolen the show for the Cubs this postseason, did what he's been doing best by dropping a double into short center field to score Heyward. Baez, a savvy baserunner for his young age, read the play all the way and made it into second base easily.

David Ross flied out to center, and with Lester at the plate, Maeda uncorked a wild pitch. The Dodgers

immediately suspected the Cubs might try to squeeze Baez home, as they held an infield meeting and brought first baseman Gonzalez in.

Lester showed bunt but did not offer. Baez had strayed off the bag, and Dodgers catcher Carlos Ruiz fired the ball to third. Baez sprinted home and beat the throw by Justin Turner. The play was scored a steal of home, the Cubs' first in a postseason game since Jimmy Slagle did so in Game 4 of the 1907 World Series.

The Wrigley Field winds did Lester no favors as the Dodgers scored a run in the fifth.

With two outs, Andre Ethier batted for Maeda and lofted a flyball to left. A south wind helped to lift it into the bleachers for a home run, cutting the Cubs' lead to 3-1. **WS**

Dexter Fowler is greeted at by Kris Bryant after his eighth-inning home run. (Steve Lundy/Daily Herald)

NATIONAL LEAGUE CHAMPIONSHIP SERIES » GAME 2

October 16, 2016 • Chicago, Illinois • Dodgers 1, Cubs 0

Ace High

Cubs Have No Answers for Kershaw, Dodgers

By Bruce Miles, dailyherald.com

In case you were wondering how Clayton Kershaw would fare in Sunday night's start against the Chicago Cubs, the answer is very well.

Kershaw, the ace of the Los Angeles Dodgers pitching staff and perhaps the best starter in the game, was coming off a closing performance in last Thursday's division series victory over the Washington Nationals. He started Game 4 of that series in Los Angeles and earned the save in Game 5.

Kershaw came out firing against the Cubs, tossing perfect baseball until Javier Baez singled with two outs in the fifth inning.

By that point, the Dodgers had a 1-0 lead, thanks to a leadoff home run in the second inning by Adrian Gonzalez off Cubs starter Kyle Hendricks. The game ended that way, and the teams will go to Dodger Stadium tied at one game apiece heading into Tuesday night's third game.

"Hitting his spots," Baez said, summing up Kershaw. "We knew he was going to pitch to us in. We just chased a lot of pitches. I honestly thought with him pitching with a couple days rest he wasn't going to be that nasty, but obviously, he came ready for us. He just did his job."

Kershaw was 12-4 with a 1.69 ERA during the regular season. He was on the disabled list from June 27-Sept. 9 with a mild herniated disc in his lower back. Against the Cubs, he wound up throwing 7 innings of 2-hit ball, with Kenley Jansen picking up a 2-inning save.

Hendricks worked 5⅓ innings giving up 3 hits. His command was a touch off, and he was up against a true ace.

"With that guy going on the other side, that's what you have to expect going into a game like that," Hendricks said. "I wasn't sharp, really. My fastball command wasn't great, but I battled through it. I really didn't miss over the plate with much. So that was good. I didn't give in. I didn't get deep into the game like I wanted to but at least kept us in the game. It was one swing away."

Getting that one swing has been a problem for several key Cubs, even if this is the playoffs and the pitching is tighter.

Anthony Rizzo was 0-for-3 with a walk. He is 1-for-23 in the postseason. Addison Russell also was 0-for-3. He is 1-for-22 in the playoffs. Jason Heyward, dropped to the No. 8 spot in the order, was 0-for-3 and his now 2-for-18.

"I feel everyone's grinding," Rizzo said. "Guys took good swings. We were just missing the ball. That's just the way the game goes sometimes. We realize we just faced the best pitcher on the planet."

The Dodgers got the early homer when Gonzalez went to the opposite field in left-center on a 1-0 pitch from Hendricks.

Once again, Baez sparkled for the Cubs on defense. In the sixth, Gonzalez walked and Josh Reddick singled with one out. Maddon replaced Hendricks with right-hander Carl Edwards Jr. to face the let-handed hitting Joc Pederson.

Pederson hit a soft liner toward Baez at second base. Baez alertly let the ball drop and threw to second base to force Reddick. The Cubs then tagged out Gonzalez in a rundown.

"As soon as the ball was hit, both of the runners went back (toward their bases)," Baez said. "I saw Pederson running down the line. I had to get one. Gonzalez came back to the bag, and I was just telling Addy (shortstop Addison Russell), 'Go three, go three, go three.'"

The Cubs had a glimmer of hope against Kershaw in the seventh. Rizzo walked to lead off. The Cubs caught a break when catcher Yasmani Grandal dropped Ben Zobrist's foul popup behind home plate.

Zobrist could not capitalize, as he struck out. Russell flied out to left. Baez came up and lined out to the warning track in center field.

"You're so used to watching a ball come off the bat, you knew it was just not far enough," said Cubs manager Joe Maddon. "You just knew it. It was hit well, then immediately you look at the outfielder and you look at the wind and you know that all inn advance. He had great at-bats. He played another excellent game." **WS**

Kris Bryant and the Cubs were kept scoreless by the Dodgers' Clayton Kershaw in Game 2. (John Starks/Daily Herald)

NATIONAL LEAGUE CHAMPIONSHIP SERIES » GAME 3

October 7, 2016 • Los Angeles, California • Dodgers 6, Cubs 0

Silenced

Hitting Slump Continues as Cubs Drop Game 3

By Bruce Miles, dailyherald.com

For the first time this year, the Chicago Cubs are up against some real adversity.

Fortunately for them, they're only a victory away from changing the narrative back in their favor again.

But for that to happen the hitters have to get going.

The Cubs were shut out for the second straight game Tuesday night as they fell 6-0 to the Los Angeles Dodgers at Dodger Stadium. The Dodgers lead the best-of-seven National League championship series two-games-to-one.

On a beautiful night in Southern California, former Cubs lefty Rich Hill was on top of his game, as he pitched 6 innings of 2-hit ball, with both hits being singles off the bat of Kris Bryant.

For many anxious Cubs fans, this series is looking like last year's NLCS, when New York Mets pitching shut down the Cubs in a four-game sweep.

"No, new team, new season," Bryant said. "I haven't really thought about last year at all. This is a very different situation, too. I felt like last year the pitching just beat us. I feel like right now, we've had some chances. We're only down 2-1. Last year at this time,

we were down three, and that's always a tough hole to climb out of. We feel fine."

Cubs manager Joe Maddon tried to breathe some life into his slumbering lineup by tweaking it. Left-handed hitting right fielder Jason Heyward sat at the start in favor of Jorge Soler, who went 0-for-1 with a walk. Maddon flip-flopped Ben Zobrist and Anthony Rizzo, moving Rizzo from third to fourth and Zobrist from cleanup to third.

Rizzo managed a broken-bat infield single in the ninth, but he is 1-for-11 in the NLCS after going 1-for-15 in the division series against the San Francisco Giants.

Maddon again pinch hit for struggling shortstop Addison Russell after Russell went hitless in 2 at-bats, making him 0-for-9 in this series after a 1-for-15 NLDS.

"We're not hitting the ball hard," said Maddon, as neither Rizzo nor Russell talked after the game. "They've pitched well. Obviously, I have no solid explanation. We've just got to keep working at it. There is really no excuse. We just have to pick it up quickly."

The Dodgers had no such problems. After winning Game 2 by a 1-0 score behind pitcher Clayton Kershaw, they scored 4 runs on 6 hits in 5 innings against Jake Arrieta.

Corey Seager had an RBI single in the third. In the fourth, Yasmani Grandal hit a 2-run homer to right-center. Arrieta's night was done when he gave up a leadoff homer to Justin Turner in the sixth.

"It was a grind," Arrieta said. "They just outplayed us on both sides tonight."

Like the rest of his mates, Arrieta was putting on his bravest face.

"I like our chances," he said. "Anytime you have a ballclub like we do, with guys with a lot of postseason experience on the mound in (John) Lackey (Wednesday night), we feel good about it. Nobody wants to be down 2-1, but at the same time, we had a really tough game against Kershaw. He pitched extremely well.

"Hill was tough on us tonight. They were pretty good offensively. They put up some really good at-bats, hit some good pitches, did a little bit more than enough to get the win against us tonight."

Hill, now 36, remains a good story. He first came up with the Cubs in 2005 as a curveball-fastball guy. After going through more downs that ups in his career, he went a combined 12-5 with a 2.12 ERA between Oakland and the Dodgers this season.

"It's the biggest game of my career, and it's all about staying in the moment and executing when you're in that moment," he said. "And that's all you can think about. And that's all you can control, is that pitch.

"But for me, looking back and getting to this point, it's just putting in the work, putting in the time, having a routine, persevere, all those things that you can kind of say sum up some kind of endurance or resiliency.

"That's all I've ever known, is just work and just continue to do the work." **WS**

Anthony Rizzo breaks his bat during the ninth inning of Game 3 against the Dodgers. (AP Photo/Jae C. Hong)

NATIONAL LEAGUE CHAMPIONSHIP SERIES » GAME 4

October 19, 2016 • Los Angeles, California • Cubs 10, Dodgers 2

Storming Back

Chicago Cubs Offense Returns in Big, Big Way to Even NLCS

By Bruce Miles, dailyherald.com

First of all, Chicago, relax.

Second of all, get ready, the National League championship series is coming back to Wrigley Field for a Game 6.

The Chicago Cubs made that possible Wednesday night, thanks to their awakening offense, as they pounded the Los Angeles Dodgers 10-2 at Dodger Stadium to even the best-of-seven NLCS at two games apiece.

Game 5 is Thursday night at Dodger Stadium. After an off-day Friday in Chicago, the two teams will play Game 6 Saturday night.

The Cubs welcomed Addison Russell and Anthony Rizzo back to the offensive fold. Russell hit a 2-run homer in the Cubs' 4-run fourth inning. Rizzo homered leading off the fifth inning and added a 2-run single in the sixth that gave the Cubs an 8-2 lead after the Dodgers came to within 5-2 in the fifth.

It seemed to be a big weight lifted off both players' shoulders. As he rounded the bases on his home run trot Russell gave a couple of little fist pumps.

Relief? Exhilaration? A little of both?

"I'd say all of the above," said Russell, who was 1-for-24 in the postseason entering the game. "I've been struggling this postseason a little bit but didn't panic. My confidence was still there. I feel like I've been seeing the ball well, taking some pretty good swings. So definitely wasn't panicking. I was a little more frustrated than anything else."

Russell went 3-for-5 in the game. Rizzo was 2-for-26 coming into Game 4. He also was 3-for-5, with 3 RBI. After a pair of strikeouts to begin Wednesday, he borrowed one of teammate Matt Szczur's bats.

"I've done it a few times, especially later in the year," he said. "Especially today, the first 2 at-bats weren't so hot."

This was a pivotal game. Had the Cubs lost, they would have faced an elimination game on the road. Now, they can go home with a 3-2 series lead with a win in Game 5 behind pitcher Jon Lester.

"I think this is a big win, for sure," Rizzo said. "With Lester going tomorrow, what he's going to bring

Addison Russell broke out of a postseason slump with a two-run home run against the Dodgers' Julio Urias. (Jae C. Hong/AP Photo)

to the table, he's going to bring the game tomorrow. In a way, this is just one game. And we know that it's going to be a quick turnaround to be ready tomorrow, but this was definitely a big game for us."

Manager Joe Maddon stuck with his regular players, putting right fielder Jason Heyward back into the lineup after not starting him Tuesday. Russell did move down to eighth in the order.

Maddon gave the start at catcher to rookie Willson Contreras, who teamed with Heyward to tag out Adrian Gonzalez trying to score the game's first run in the third inning.

"Yeah, that's our team," Maddon said. "You saw our team out there today. We scuffled in the beginning there."

The Cubs cranked out 13 hits and got great bullpen work after starting pitcher John Lackey went only 4 innings for the second time in the postseason.

In the bottom of the fifth, Lackey walked the first two batters, so Maddon wen to lefty Mike Montgomery, who allowed a 2-run single to Justin Turner.

Montgomery was the victim of his own bad luck as he deflected Turner's ball and sent what could have been a double-play bouncer into left field. But he shut the Dodgers down after that and got the win with 2 innings of shutout ball.

As always, Maddon was upbeat about the baseball.

"What you've seen so far, it's been a pretty interesting series to this point," he said. "I did not expect it to be such a lopsided victory for us today. Tomorrow will be a pretty nice day to come out on top and, going back home, having to win one of two. We've been pretty good at Wrigley all year. So it's just an interesting baseball series, man. I think it's great. I think it's great for baseball." **WS**

Top: Willson Contreras tags out Adrian Gonzalez at home during the second inning of Game 4. (Mark J. Terrill/AP Photo) Opposite: Anthony Rizzo is congratulated by Javier Baez after his fifth-inning home run widened the Cubs' lead. (David J. Phillip/AP Photo)

NATIONAL LEAGUE CHAMPIONSHIP SERIES » GAME 5

October 20, 2016 • Los Angeles, California • Cubs 8, Dodgers 4

One Win Away

Lester Pitches Cubs to the Brink

By Barry Rozner, dailyherald.com

Since last reaching the World Series 71 years ago, only twice have the Cubs come within a game of reaching the World Series.

After Thursday night, you can make it three.

The Cubs had three chances to get it done in 1984 and three more in 2003, and both times the dream ended with three consecutive defeats.

Now, thanks to Jon Lester and Addison Russell, they've got a pair of games to get it done — and one of them involves Clayton Kershaw.

So after giving away home-field advantage in a Game 2 loss to Kershaw at Wrigley Field Sunday, the Cubs did just what they needed to do, which was take two of three in Los Angeles and give themselves two opportunities in Chicago to advance to the Fall Classic.

But it was far from easy.

After getting nothing done offensively in Games 2 and 3, the Cubs busted out in Game 4 and left it up to Lester in Game 5, an appropriate spot for the $155 million man brought in to serve as the veteran ace who's been in these tough postseason spots so many times before.

And rather than start Kershaw in Game 5, Dodgers manager Dave Roberts gambled that he could get enough out of starter Kenta Maeda to get to his bullpen before the Cubs put a big number on the board, and it looked like the visitors would get that big number early.

But it was only 1-0 Cubs when Roberts yanked Maeda in the top of the fourth, and when the Dodgers tied it at 1-1 in the bottom of the inning, Roberts' gamble looked like it might pay off, mostly because the Cubs left runners in scoring position in the first, fourth and fifth.

Still, the problem with relying on a bullpen day after day in the postseason is all you need is one guy to be out of sync and it can cost you a game.

Or maybe more.

That happened to the Dodgers when Javy Baez led off the sixth with a base hit against Joe Blanton and stole second. With one out, Russell blasted his second

Jon Lester gave the Cubs seven strong innings in an emphatic Game 5 start. (Mark J. Terrill/AP Photo)

homer in as many days and the Cubs had a 3-1 lead with Lester at only 79 pitches through 5 innings.

Would Roberts have been better off with Kershaw? Well, at that point Blanton had given up 3 homers and 2 doubles in his last 8 hitters.

Meanwhile, Lester cruised through the sixth and in the seventh he worked past a two-out base hit and finished 7 strong innings at 107 pitches, having allowed just a run on 5 hits with a walk and 6 strikeouts.

He gave the Cubs exactly what they needed in Game 5.

It's true that the Cubs were awful with runners in scoring position Thursday night, but in the top of the eighth with two on and one out, Dexter Fowler and Kris Bryant both delivered infield hits that made it 5-1 Cubs, and though it might not have been very loud, those extra runs were thunder in the ears of the Dodgers.

Baez then cleared the bases with a double and the Cubs had an 8-1 lead.

So after zero runs for two games, the Cubs came up with some big numbers in the last two and they have pushed the Dodgers to another elimination game.

Down 2-1 in the NLDS against Washington, Los Angeles won two straight to survive the Nats, Kershaw starting the first one and saving the second two days later.

This time, he'll have to win Game 6 and likely be unavailable for Game 7, though you never know.

In any case, the Cubs displayed some serious guts on the road and now they're just one game away from getting to the big dance, a goal they have talked about since being eliminated by the Mets.

After what they did in L.A., it might be a mistake to doubt them now. **WS**

Top: Javier Baez rounds first on his way to a 2-run double. (Jae C. Hong/AP Photo) Opposite: Addison Russell is congratulated in the dugout after scoring during the eighth inning. (Mark J. Terrill)

History in the Making

Cubs Defy Odds, History With Pennant

By Barry Rozner, dailyherald.com

Almost any Cubs fan will default to the odds, an understandable resignation given the circumstances.

Nearly every one of you has set the wager at a billion-to-1, the chances of the team ever reaching the World Series in your lifetime.

But it wasn't actually quite that high.

If you go back to 2011, the Red Sox had just a 0.3 percent chance of failing to make the playoffs on Sept. 3.

On Sept. 28, 2011, the Rays had just a 0.3 percent chance of coming back after trailing 7-0 with 2 innings to play.

The Red Sox had only a 2 percent chance of losing their game against Baltimore that night, when the Orioles were down to their last strike.

The Rays had a 2 percent chance of winning in the bottom of the 9th, with Dan Johnson also down to his last strike before his monumental, game-tying home run.

Multiply all four together, and according to noted mathematician Nate Silver, you get a combined probability of one chance in 278 million that of all those events would occur, coming together at once and creating the greatest night in baseball history.

It created something else rather significant. It created the 2016 Chicago Cubs.

If the Red Sox had made the 2011 playoffs, Terry Francona would not have been fired. If he hadn't been fired, Theo Epstein never would have left Boston.

But the Red Sox crumbled, Francona got his pink slip and the Cubs at that very moment just happened to be looking for someone to take over their baseball operation.

Yup, 278-million-to-1. So much for the odds.

"Baseball is a funny game," Epstein said. "And life can be funny, too. No one could have possibly predicted all of this."

Epstein's Cubs reached the World Series for the first time since 1945 Saturday at 9:45 p.m. and touched off a party in Wrigleyville unlike any ever seen in these parts.

With apologies to Jon Bon Jovi and all who have hit their knees in the last seven decades, the Cubs are

Anthony Rizzo, Kris Bryant, Addison Russell, and Javier Baez celebrate earning their spot in the World Series. (Steve Lundy/Daily Herald)

halfway there -- and it has little to do with livin' on a prayer.

It has everything to do with a plan, a plan that was mocked and derided by the cynics incapable of seeing past the obtuseness of it all.

Not that Epstein cared.

The man had a formula for building a World Series team. He just didn't imagine he could do it from scratch in five years.

But he has done precisely that -- and now the Cubs are halfway to a dream season.

The magic number is 4.

"It's great to be this far and we celebrate that," Epstein said. "We'll get back to business soon because we have unfinished business, but we'll take this tonight and make sure we celebrate that."

For the thousands who have waited since 1945 to say they saw the Cubs in the World Series again, and for the millions who have doubted they would witness it, this is a wondrous and bewildering occasion.

The Cubs are built to last, young and good and sustainable -- many bites at the apple, as it were -- but there are no guarantees of a return engagement, so halfway there is not enough.

It is not nearly enough.

And it's too painful to consider the downside, because as the Bears proved in 2006, getting there and losing is worse than not getting there at all.

So now comes the real pressure -- and maybe the real pleasure.

Celebrate they may, and celebrate they have, but come what may the Cubs must win the World Series or face the unkindest of music, the most cruel of jokes.

No one wants to say the Cubs finally made it to a World Series, and, of course, lost.

The Cubs got there Saturday night at Wrigley Field before 42,386 crazed fanatics, and they did it against the very best there is, Clayton Kershaw.

The Dodgers monster starter looked uncomfortable

from the beginning and the Cubs had good swings throughout Kershaw's 5 innings, posting 5 runs on 7 hits and a couple of home runs. They also got a few breaks along the way, perhaps cashing in on a century's worth they've saved up.

At the same time, Kyle Hendricks was absolutely brilliant, forcing more Greg Maddux comparisons, keeping the Dodgers off balance and breezing through 7⅓ strong innings on only 2 hits.

When Aroldis Chapman got the final out for a 5-0 victory, Cubs players, execs and families poured out onto the field and celebrated with the faithful, who endured this rebuild and got their reward Saturday.

But the Cubs to a man say that they have not reached their goal, that the Cleveland Indians await and that the real test has not yet been taken.

In less than two weeks, they hope to tell a very different story.

So if you made a deal with the Devil Saturday morning, if you sold your tortured soul for a chance to see the Cubs in a World Series, this is your time.

Pay up and enjoy the next 11 days, because it won't get any hotter than this.

Rejoice Chicago, you're four wins away from the real party. **WS**

Top: A Cubs fan shows of a sign after a 5-0 victory to clinch the National League pennant. Opposite: Anthony Rizzo waves a flag after the Cubs beat the Dodgers in Game 6. (Steve Lundy/Daily Herald)

For the Ages

'Cubs' and 'World Series' Finally Belong in Same Sentence

Mike Imrem, dailyherald.com | October 23, 2016

Full disclosure: I had no right to moan that the Cubs never won anything in my lifetime.

I was seven months old the last time they won a National League pennant.

It's difficult to remember too much about it but all these years later I'm able to use "Cubs" and "World Series" in the same sentence without drawing snickers.

My fingers barely can type it, my head barely can comprehend it: The Cubs are in the World Series for the first time since 1945.

No, seriously, it's true after the Cubs disposed of the Dodgers 5-0 in Saturday night's Game 6 of the NLCS before a raucous hockey-style crowd in Wrigley Field.

The Cubs exorcised the demons of not winning a National League pennant in 71 years. Starting Tuesday at Cleveland they have a chance to exorcise the demons of not winning a World Series in 108 years.

It was exhilarating to stand and watch the Cubs jump around on the middle of the infield to celebrate their newly minted pennant.

You don't have to be a Cubs fan to recognize the magnitude of this, right, White Sox fans?

I expected to live to 100 or 1,000 or forever without seeing the Cubs play a World Series game.

What I just saw was so surreal that my entire life as a Chicago baseball fan flashed before my eyes.

For starters, my parents took me to Wrigley Field for the first time at age 5. Walking up through the tunnel into the grandstands, it was awesome how bright everything was.

Moving on, I'm thinking of my friend's father who painted apartments in Logan Square. During the summer he scheduled jobs for when the Cubs were on road trips so he could take us to the ballpark during homestands.

Then there's the older man who stocked shelves in a neighborhood drugstore. He always happened to be working near the radio when Cub games were on.

Look, there's my older brother taking me to the ballpark. We were first in line at the bleacher gate, raced up to get front-row seats and tossed packs of gum

Fans at Wrigley Field celebrate after the Cubs beat the Dodgers to advance to the World Series. (Steve Lundy/Daily Herald)

down to Hank Sauer because we weren't old enough to buy him chewing tobacco.

So many of those folks left us without ever seeing the Cubs win a pennant.

Today they're up somewhere listening to late broadcasters Jack Quinlan, Jack Brickhouse, Lou Boudreau, Vince Lloyd and Harry Caray capturing Saturday night's milestone.

My goodness, Ron Santo lived for this day before dying without witnessing it. Ernie Banks didn't live long enough to say, "The Cubs got their kicks in 2-0-1-6!"

Bless all the Cub fans who on their deathbeds sighed, "The Cubs are killing me."

For seven decades, as bouncing babies aged into senior citizens, the Cubs couldn't advance to a World Series.

No wonder it has been easy for me to remember all the close calls, starting with sitting in the right-field bleachers as the Cubs soared in 1969 and on a bar stool at Keystone Liquors as they came crashing down.

Among other teases were the free-fall of 1977, the Gatorade glove of '84 and the collapse of '03.

Curses!

Now the Cubs and their fans are celebrating a National League pennant.

Ponder that a moment ... the Cubs and their fans are celebrating a National League pennant.

All the Cubs have to do from here is win the World Series to complete the journey of a lifetime. **WS**

Opposite: Carl Edwards Jr. carries the 'W' flag after the Cubs' Game 6 NLCS triumph. (Steve Lundy/Daily Herald) Top: For the first time in over a century, Cubs fans in 2016 got to check all three boxes. (John Starks/Daily Herald)

(Steve Lundy/Daily Herald)